Making Data Work

Making Data Work

Enabling Digital Transformation, Empowering People and Advancing Organisational Success

Edosa Odaro

CRC Press
Taylor & Francis Group
Boca Raton London New York

CRC Press is an imprint of the
Taylor & Francis Group, an **informa** business

AN AUERBACH BOOK

First edition published 2022

by CRC Press
6000 Broken Sound Parkway NW, Suite 300, Boca Raton, FL 33487-2742

and by CRC Press
4 Park Square, Milton Park, Abingdon, Oxon, OX14 4RN

ISBN: 978-1-032-23192-1 (hbk)
ISBN: 978-1-032-22443-5 (pbk)
ISBN: 978-1-003-27827-6 (ebk)

DOI: 10.1201/9781003278276

Typeset in Minion
by SPi Technologies India Pvt Ltd (Straive)

This book reflects the author's present recollections of experiences over time. Some names of persons and organisations have been changed to protect their privacy. Some events and dialogues have been compressed.

To my late mum. You touched the lives of so many. You continue to guide me in all my earthly endeavours and to inspire my drive to create positive change.

Contents

PART IV Bringing It All Together: Exposing Recombinant Evolutions of Technical Solutions and Their Practical Applications

Endorsements for *Making Data Work*

Odaro has penned a book – based on a broad and important experience in the world of data – that is packed with real-life stories and conversations that give the reader plenty of food for thought in areas they may not have seen themselves. In a market with lots of "data books," this one stands out as it does not purport to have the silver bullet but instead leads with business situations and links them to the data issues and strategies that could help solve them. This makes it an accessible and enjoyable read which puts us "in the room" of some of the most significant data challenges in recent times.

– Barry Panayi,
Director of Data, Insights and Analytics at John Lewis Partnership

This timely book exposes powerful examples of the root causes of data challenges and provides deep insights into their implications for businesses. It is a wake-up call that not only highlights where things go wrong but also provides invaluable insights into how to make data work. Edosa's insights are invaluable for every leader of today.

– Gunilla Svensson, CEO at Dina Forsakringar

At last, the quintessential voice of an accomplished Chief Data Officer has spoken and opens up the stage doors for more award-winning CDOs to join the conversation. In this groundbreaking work, Edosa clearly places Chief Data Officers in the driving seat of the dialogue. A counterweight to the many other voices telling us, about "who we are" and "what value we bring." At this crucial time in history, the world desperately needs to build back stronger from the ills of the pandemic and tackle our climate challenges, yet, the airwaves are cluttered with "white noise" from authors with insufficient depth or breadth in data. This essential work cuts through the noise and brings crystal clarity. Its unique perspective simplifies seemingly impossible data problems through real-life storytelling. It exposes the world of data to business people – without the need to become a data geek. Ultimately, this book tells you how to make the shift from "data as a liability" to "data as an asset" for your organisation.

– Althea Davis, Managing Partner and Chief Data Officer at Avantologie, Board of Directors at the International Society of Chief Data Officers (isCDO), CDO Magazine's 2021 Power Data Woman. CDO Magazine's, Editorial Board Member and Chairwoman, MEA Region

Easy to read and packed with relatable examples, "Making Data Work" is a must-read for data professionals and business leaders who want to understand what truly hinders digital transformations, and how to get past the seemingly impossible blockers!

– Dora Boussias, Director Enterprise Architecture & Data Strategy at Stryker

With a fresh approach to the world of data, Edosa throws light on the challenges associated with the complex network of silos present in organisations, with an insightful, personal and enjoyable account of the challenges of the data supply chain and the enormous potential of using data intelligently within businesses.

– Julie Wall, Director of Impact and Innovation for the School of Architecture, Computing and Engineering at the University of East London

Immersive storytelling at its best, Edosa takes the reader on a personal journey through his diverse professional experience, operating across multiple industries and cultures in the data space and provides a unique blend of creative and valuable insights into how to make data work. A recommended read for any data or transformation professional.

– Mike Eggington, Head of Engineering at AXA

Edosa brings extensive real-life experience to paper in this book, providing the ideal guide for aspiring and incumbent data leaders.

– Dr. Akinola Akinyemi, Head of Data Science at IG

The potential for artificial intelligence to enhance the success of organisations and add value to the wider society is ever increasing. Yet, this potential is significantly hampered by the persistence of ubiquitous data challenges. This book offers unique insights into the sources of such challenges and provides experienced-based solutions on how they can be overcome.

– Ibra Diouf, Startup Success at Google

In this book, Edosa presents a thought-provoking, evidence-led and insightful exposé which covers crucial aspects of the data dimension in a modern global organisation from preserving data integrity to ensuring completeness, sound governance and disclosure. He brings in an entirely refreshing perspective into the conversation. It is a must-read for every business leader, CDAO and their team.

– Dr. Seun Ajao (PhD, FHEA), Course Leader, MSc. Data Analytics with Banking and Finance at Sheffield Hallam University

This book is an absolute must-read for business leaders, data practitioners and technologists. Edosa's style is engaging and is delivered through deeply relatable and contemporary stories. This book is thought-provoking, helpful and inspirational.

– David Stern, Data Engineer formerly at Sony

"Making Data Work" is the most insightful and engaging book on data-driven digital transformation I've had the privilege to read. It provides an insider's guide to developing an effective data-driven culture with a unique real-world strategy for exploiting the disruptive power of artificial intelligence to transform your company's future. It takes you through Edosa's personal journey using masterful storytelling to share his hard-won insights. The book presents rich case studies of transformation, talent management, paradigm shifts, culture, data and the organisational silo conundrum. Moving from failure and finally incredible success in transforming business performance with data, this book highlights the persistence of ubiquitous data challenges and what organisations and people can do about them. It also provides a comprehensive list of potential solutions for those challenges. This book is an absolute must-read for making data work for you.

– Dante Healy, Agile Finance Transformation Specialist

Easy to read, yet plenty of sharp thoughts for data practitioners wherever they are in their journey. If you are passionate about data, if you like a dialogue with your peers, if you want to see some of our common experiences from a unique angle, then you will surely enjoy reading this book!

– Santiago Castro, Chief Data Officer at FBN Bank

A must-read for anybody who wants to thrive in an increasingly data-centric world.

– Dr Kemal Ahson, Faculty of Educational Sciences at the
University of Helsinki

Avoiding technical jargon, Edosa highlights challenges that no data professional can afford to ignore. The engaging and entertaining examples he gives of business successes and failures are turned into practical advice building on Edosa's extensive professional experience as well as his deep understanding of cultural contexts. This book is packed with invaluable takeaways and insights for data practitioners across all verticals.

– Dr. Bertie Muller, Programme Director for Computer Science at
Swansea University

This timely book exposes powerful examples of the root causes of where data can hit challenges. Edosa has clearly detailed how you can create opportunities for your business to leverage data, overcome the roadblocks and use it to add exceptional value to your team and clients. This book is one you NEED to delve into if you want to learn how to maximise the data you have with proven frameworks, questions and considerations for incredible success with data.

– Tom Allen, Founder at the AI Journal

A timely book, offering practical advice on how to recognise and address the organisational issues that hamper flows of data, information and knowledge. Edosa Odaro has written convincingly from personal experience, placing as much emphasis on people as he does on the role of transformational technology.

– Alan Smith OBE, Head of Visual and Data Journalism at the
Financial Times

There can be no doubt of the increasing importance of data to companies and to individuals, yet too many organisations struggle to leverage its full potential. This book shifts focus from status quo solutions such as acquiring more resources and building new processes but instead exposes success stories that focus on peeling back old strategies and being unafraid to confront the status quo.

– Louise Gray, Head of Digital in Life Management at the DWP

Uplifting! This book written by the knowledgeable expert in data, that is Edosa, is a compendium of concrete solutions to efficiently get the most out of your data.

– Franck ELLA, Head of Data at AXA Direct France

While data is central to digital transformation, transforming the mindset of people and driving organisational change is key to its success. How to make it work? Edosa is leading us by exposing unique and valuable insights gained from his personal and professional journey, across continents and across industries. Inspirational. Practical. Don't miss out.

– Mathieu Roozekrans,
Director of Product Lifecycle at NX P Semiconductors

In a captivating recollection of real-life situations, Edosa's book offers a rare glimpse into the challenges faced by leaders in data departments everywhere. I highly recommend it to those seeking actionable advice on how to steer their data strategy and deliver measurable impact for their broader organisation.

– George Ciobanu, Machine Learning Engineering Consultant

It turns out that data can work for us or even against us. Edosa provides many real-world examples, including on how organisations look at silos, and shares powerful design principles for "making data work."

– Paul Merila,
Senior Information Technology Consultant at EPAM Systems

This book offers fresh insight into how to solve the interactional frictions that hamper the flow of data, information and knowledge across organisations. Yet, rather than being stuck with endless polarising debates, such as breaking down silos, it shifts focus back towards the ultimate "to what end."

– Jacky Wright, Chief Digital Officer (CDO) at Microsoft U.S.

If you care about AI transformation, empowering people or advancing organisational success in an increasingly digital world, then you should read this book.

– Yomi Ibosiola, Chief Data and Analytics Officer at Union Bank

In this book, Edosa explores common challenges which limit the value that organisations can get from data. What makes his book unique is that he also tackles one of the unspoken barriers to data adoption – fear. Fear of the unknown, fear of the intangible, fear of the investment needed and, yes, fear of losing your job to a machine. With his talent for distilling clarity from complexity, Edosa tackles this and many other challenges.

– Tim Carmichael, Chief Data Officer at Chalhoub Group

Acknowledgements

The insights that inspired *Making Data Work* come from a wide range of experiences that I have had the privilege of gaining over the past 20 years of working with incredibly talented people across some iconic brands. I am therefore very grateful to my colleagues and leaders from AXA, Allianz, TaP, Barclays Group, Flutter Entertainment Betfair, British Sky Broadcasting, JLL, the European Commission, DEFRA, Lloyds Banking Group, HMRC, Severn Trent Water, Marsh, CitiGroup Egg Bank, Channel 4, Lloyds TSB, Liverpool Victoria's LV and AIG, where I currently work. I am also fortunate to currently sit with some incredible minds on the boards of Harper Adams University and the U.K.'s national institute for health data science (HDR U.K.).

I am deeply grateful to Susanne Martin whose role went far beyond being my editor to being a coach and friend and providing a level of accountability that helped to bring this work to fruition.

I am also most appreciative of the feedback from my beta readers, who not only took precious time out of their challenging schedules to review an unfinished work but also went many steps further – to provide the invaluable tough love needed to refine this book to the best it can be.

My acknowledgement would be incomplete without the mention of John Wyzalek, my acquiring editor, who connected with my story very early on and was immeasurably supportive throughout the journey to publication.

Yet my deepest debt of gratitude must go to my friends and family. To my friends, for being an ever-present source of encouragement and helping me step away from it all whenever that was needed. To my father and siblings: without your critique, support and encouragement, this would never have happened. To my young children, my nieces and nephews, who through it all provided a powerful motivation for actively modelling the kind of world we would hope we can build for the future. Most of all, to my wife who is my greatest critic but also my biggest supporter, for being there when I needed a shoulder to lean on but also for creating the space required for enabling this work to progress by making significant sacrifices in family time and by taking on far more than her fair share to enable the continuation of those essential things that we too often take for granted.

Author

Edosa Odaro is global cross-industry AI and data transformation leader and a mastermind behind several innovations that have resulted in organisational success thanks to the effective implementation of data transformation strategies. In leadership positions across diverse sectors, he has helped over 35 leading international organisations deliver significant impact through analytics and intelligent interventions.

As a Nigerian-born data specialist with an academic background in economics, computer science, business, technology and innovation, Edosa is a firm believer in the importance of a significant focus on people and on culture as well as a brand of inclusion that is underpinned by the diversity of minds. From his vast store of meticulous field notes and interview transcripts chronicling 23 years of experience, he has compiled a record of insights and methodologies never before presented.

A keen advocate for diversity and an experienced presenter and speaker, Edosa has been named a Financial Times Top 100 Most Influential Leader and one of the U.K.'s 30 Most Influential Black Leaders in FinTech.

Beyond the world of work, Edosa enjoys spending time with his wife and two sons – experiencing a variety of activities, including football, cycling, running and skiing.

Introduction

In terms of data processing capacity, it is hard to imagine a system as complex, capable and efficient as the human brain, where synaptic connections allow us to tap into a vast depository of thoughts, decisions and memories – both lived and learned – to arrive at insights that may be both personally and universally applicable at the same time.

It is fitting that one such memory – which represents a starting point in my quest to look at the interplay of technological and environmental factors in data transformation – should serve to connect my professional life to my place of origin.

My recollection of that long-ago moment is still vivid. I can smell the sweet aroma of suya, a uniquely spiced, lean-yet-succulent beef dish, cooked on an open coal barbecue. Miles away from the vendor handing me the satisfying snack, the smell lingers in the car that is taking me to Lagos International Airport, from where my flight to London will depart shortly.

The sated feeling from the meal wears off as traffic slows to a crawl and eventually comes to a complete standstill. As the driver navigates through Marina, the city's financial district, I see the usual hawkers trying to take advantage of the gridlock to tout their wares. Even a sudden torrential downpour doesn't dampen their persistence. Just ahead of us, there is a woman with a baby tied to her back and a pyramid of tomatoes balanced on her head, who narrowly escapes being knocked over by one of the notorious motorcycle taxis – locally called Okada – that often zip through the razor-thin spaces between cars.

As I contemplate the vibrant surroundings to take my mind off the worry about missing my flight, a radio announcement disrupts my thoughts.

News is just coming through to us from the Reuters news agency: the top U.S. investment bank – the Lehman Brothers – has just filed for bankruptcy protection.

I lean forward in my seat, contemplating the impact of this historic event, which would later become known as the trigger of the Great Recession.

It fuels my impatience to get back to London and immerse myself in a milieu that promises close engagement with this inflection point, yet I cannot help but wonder what repercussions may be in store for the people who populate the colourful scene around me and who, for the most part, are still oblivious to that ripple on the other end of the world that would turn into a tsunami affecting financial systems globally.

In the aftermath of the taxi ride, which brought me to the plane just in time due to a sudden shift in the flow of traffic, I was thrust into the centre of efforts to mitigate the crisis.

Data, it was felt, would provide the answer. Data would not only point the way out of the current predicament but inform better means for protection going forward.

As I progressed along a career path centred on data transformation, I again and again encountered the belief that data – and the technology enabling it – were key to solving a range of challenges in widely diverse fields and circumstances. Fast-forward to today when, in spite of the peak of the coronavirus pandemic being far behind us, organisations are still dealing with its outfalls which forced a wholesale shift towards digital engagement and remote working, again relying on technology and digital data infrastructures.

Data landscapes are complex. They are influenced by a large number of factors – and not all of them are technological in nature. I learned that an overly narrow view of the situation – one that doesn't take external factors into account – will likely lead to a dead end that doesn't yield viable solutions or perhaps brings answers that only work in the short term.

Drawing on examples from my extensive experience gained in the intervening years, I felt compelled to share insights on what works and what doesn't – rooted in concrete situations.

One scenario at an insurance company, for example, culminated in a 3:30 a.m. call on a Saturday morning. I picked up to find myself confronted with a nightmare situation. As a recently appointed head of data, I was informed that an entire critical service stream in our production systems had crashed. This critical issue meant that the central motor insurance database relied upon by law enforcement agencies had not been updated. Shock turned to horror when I found that these failures had led to legitimate customers – who had recently bought car insurance policies from us – being detained by the police. Due to our service failure, the authorities had found no record of valid insurance policies in the database for the cars they were driving. Investigations later revealed that avoidable information gaps across support teams and systems were at the root of the mayhem – and had rendered team members powerless to avoid catastrophe.

As I contemplated this ordeal in the days and the weeks that followed, it became clear that this was no isolated incident. In fact, it was reminiscent of patterns I had seen recur through my interactions with over 20 household brands over the years.

In one scenario, a retail giant already struggling due to the Covid-19 pandemic was faced with a disastrous situation when – at the end of a critical investment in an artificial intelligence project that had been meant to save money – it suddenly discovered that its implementation was likely to leave it worse off.

In another scenario very early in my career, I saw a well-planned data and insurance service migration come to a dramatic failure on the Easter weekend it was supposed to be delivered to customers.

In yet another case, I witnessed the significant pressure of a very high-profile multilateral project failing to deliver its globally and publicly committed outcome.

And another situation saw an exceptionally innovative firm struggling to keep up with its customer growth and almost coming to its knees.

Perhaps the most spectacular of these examples was the implication of such unfortunate failures I witnessed at the point when the financial giant, the Lehman Brothers, tipped the entire global financial industry into chaos.

Making Data Work is an attempt to understand what lies beneath this recurring pattern – and what the incredible potential that data, artificial intelligence and advanced technological developments can contribute to the success of organisations. It is also an opportunity to explore factors that seem to hamper the efforts of otherwise incredibly capable individuals and organisations.

Beyond the exploration of such ubiquitous challenges, this book draws on my experiences over the past two decades and exposes the approaches that have worked – and those that have not. It reveals battles between stakeholder camps and between technology factions. It considered the implications of silos, in terms of data and technology but also in terms of people and organisations. It considered the perspectives of the *hold-firm* camps that seem extremely cautious and that espouse the benefits of maintaining the status quo. It also interrogates the viewpoints of the *demolish-all* camps who seem razor-focused on outcomes and embrace the ideology of a "results at all cost" mindset underpinned by radical increases in the speed of change.

While both sides present some strong and valid positions – they seem to represent an impossible coexistence.

This book is a journey to determine what to do to "make data work" for ourselves and for our organisations. And as there are unmistakably strong benefits on both sides of the coin, it is a journey to discover how to "bring it all together." It is not only packed with case studies on what approaches do not work but also provides actionable solutions that have delivered desirable outcomes.

Beyond observed hostilities and skirmishes among determined factions and unyielding camps, it is clear that the world wants much more – that we want much more. We want a world where data and technology finally live up to the hype and deliver better human outcomes, where artificial intelligence can move us from reacting to certain situations to predicting future scenarios and possibilities. We want a world that enables positive implications for our health, for our climate and for our financial well-being – one that could go even further to leverage the combined effects of predictive artificial intelligence and prescriptive intelligent interventions to create a world where most distressing accidents and losses could be avoided altogether.

Yet over the years, we seem to have become sufficiently accepting of the status quo and of the less-than-optimal outcomes it delivers. Such understandable complacency enables most of us to leave the most challenging of conundrums unanswered while we move onto other things.

This book comes out of my refusal to simply accept the status quo.

Part I

Stakes Beyond Borders

Encountering Implications of Data Challenges on a Global Scale

1

A Crossfire of Consternation

The hustle and bustle on the London subway platform was what you would expect during a week-day rush hour. Anxious commuters pushed their way forward as trains came and went, allowing only two or three passengers to squeeze their way into the already full compartments at a time. I let myself be carried along with the bodies crowding around me, deep in thought about the day's meeting with bankers and financial regulators. Although both sides were eager to map out a way forward from the Lehman Brothers crash that had tipped the entire global financial industry into chaos – and both saw data and analytics as key to stabilising the situation, consensus seemed a far way off when it came to implementing concrete strategies.

Still reeling from the clash I had witnessed in the boardroom of BBG, a global banking organisation where I worked as head of data, I looked around me with new appreciation for the increasingly data-driven world we were living in.

Never before had I considered that data could be so critically important for the functioning of the global banking sector, which was worth over 90 trillion dollars, as well as our day-to-day lives and livelihoods that were intrinsically dependent on the effective functioning of the financial system.

Could data really help to get us out of this mess? I wondered as I pulled my coat closer around me and waited for the next train to arrive. I couldn't quite land on an answer, as my brain was still foggy from a sleepless night, which had come to an abrupt end with the ringing of my alarm at 5:45 a.m.

There had been no shortage of thoughts floating through my mind while I lay awake, with a piece of research about brains I had recently picked up prominent among them. Contemporary science suggests that our brains are the single largest data stores in the world. I had been particularly intrigued

DOI: 10.1201/9781003278276-2

to learn that while the neurons – the brain cells primarily responsible for storage, processing and transportation of information – have sufficient capacity to store our movie needs for the next couple of years, the synapses, which are the bridges that facilitate the connections between these neurons, enable an exponential increase in this capacity. They allow our brains to store over 300 years of continuous Netflix video streaming. The Stanford University study did, however, go on to suggest that most of our stored memories lie in a passive and dormant state with only a handful of the most striking events occupying prominence in the front of our minds.

One such indelible memory came from the meeting that was sandwiched between that sleepless night and my journey home.

I had been standing by the boardroom window of one of the world's largest financial institutions with Fred, one of its most powerful senior executive leaders.

"Most ordinary people, like you and me, are in no doubt that we are not built to last forever," he said without shifting his gaze from the incredible panoramic view across Canary Wharf, the City of London and the entire Financial District. "Most of us also consider that we would rather predetermine how our financial matters are resolved when we are no more. We take it upon ourselves to write a will."

As he slowly turned towards me, he continued, "Yet large global organisations like ours – who employ hundreds of thousands of people and manage the finances of millions more – have never stopped to consider what might happen if they ceased to be a going concern."

It was an incredible analogy to make. Indeed, the big question was how a global meltdown of that scale had been allowed to happen.

Financial crises were not a novel occurrence. For centuries, history has been shaped by economic cycles in which busts followed booms. Records place the earliest notable crisis during the Emperor Tiberius' frugal rule of the Roman Empire in the 1st century, when he gained fame for employing sophisticated quantitative easing measures to restore order and bring the economy to a point of recovery. There was also the Credit Crisis of 1772. It was triggered by a run-on a bank in London and soon spread across the United Kingdom and into Europe. The 1997 Asian Crisis originated in Thailand, from where it engulfed the rest of the East Asian Tiger economies of Thailand, Indonesia, Malaysia, Singapore, Hong Kong and South Korea.

However, the Great Depression is perhaps the most notable event on record. Starting on "Black Thursday," the 24th of October in 1929, it lasted over ten years, led to a worldwide economic depression, forced unemployment rates up to 25 per cent, and slashed the U.S. GDP by 50 per cent.

Yet the Great Recession of 2007 was distinctly different. Triggered by the sudden collapse of the U.S. subprime housing bubble and accelerated by the shocking demise of Lehman Brothers, one of the oldest and largest investment banking corporations in the world, it had already led to global stock markets descending into free fall, job cuts being announced in the thousands and unprecedented government bailout packages being released in the billions and trillions.

Given the devastating effects of financial crises on global political economies, national governments and policymakers have long been motivated to pursue policy measures to ensure financial stability. The goal for implementing such policy measures – together with associated mechanisms and tools – was to avoid or reduce the potentially cataclysmic economic consequences of financial volatility. Central banks serve such a purpose – to maintain a stable financial system and mitigate risks of a systemic failure across the financial landscape.

Most national governments establish such financial structures not only to provide an appropriate level of oversight – to ensure that monetary transactions travel securely through the system and are effectively settled at their intended destinations – but also to avert any risk of liquidity exiguity, especially in the event of a financial crisis.

However, despite the abundance of structures and efforts that global economies dedicate to mitigating such risks, I found that nothing could galvanise action like an imminent or an actual failure. Beyond the Great Recession, which seemed to consume our entire attention at its peak, I noticed that an intrinsic relationship between failure and action was by no means limited to the financial sector or the world of work. Instead, it was evident in our everyday lives, in the big as well as the small.

A recent example of this comes from the coronavirus pandemic. There were extensive risk analyses and warnings – including an impassioned TED Talk by Bill Gates – that stressed the need for being prepared and for employing early mitigation measures to avoid the most devastating outcomes. However, most governments and organisations across the globe only took decisive action when a failure was imminent – and when data indicated that the pandemic was at their doorstep.

My journey towards understanding what it takes to make data work took a notable leap forward when I investigated what went wrong in the financial crisis when I pondered how Lehman Brothers could have evaded all the controls of the collection of central banks across the globe. Beyond understanding the connection between failure and action, I was keen to unpick how we can leverage data insights not only for mitigation but also to prevent detrimental events.

It was difficult to imagine how an organisation of the size and scale of Lehman Brothers could actually operate without the sort of basic provisions that most people make to predetermine the resolution of their financial affairs. Explicitly articulated wills, trusts and insurances are typical tools individuals employ, yet it seemed that such planning was left wanting for some of the largest organisations in the world. Contemplated more broadly, it wasn't just the survival of an individual organisation that was at stake. Instead, its complex financial affairs were suboptimally encoded so that a complicated and difficult-to-untangle maze was left behind.

The news was awash with headlines suggesting that, going forward, financial institutions should be compelled to publicly disclose their ability to pay up and address any liabilities they might have should they come to a situation of inevitable failure where they would need to be wound down. "U.K. banks will have to publish 'living wills' to ensure 'orderly failure,'" one headline declared. It was clear that the Bank of England and other financial regulators across the globe were very concerned about the implications of the failure of large banks for the broader economy. They were desperate to reduce the chances of the kinds of bailouts the taxpayer had been compelled to fund.

As our conversation in BBG's boardroom progressed, Fred was keen to go beyond disclosure and delve deeper into the broader role of data.

"What is your view?" he asked.

> Are you here to convince me that data or AI are the answer, that data can be the ultimate mitigant for future financial systemic failures? And what we need is to funnel all our data into a super-sized Hadoop data lake?

"There is no doubt that data has to play a huge role, and advancements in artificial intelligence would only act to radically increase the utility achievable from data," I said. "But I think the situation is a lot more nuanced than simply getting access to more data."

I pointed out that there had been a lot of attention on data by global financial rule-setters in the past. A recent example was the Basel II Framework, which was already in force at the point of the crash. It placed data at the heart of its market discipline reforms – and its three pillars stressed the critical importance of information disclosure to the well-being of the financial system.

"Yes," Fred said, acknowledging that such regulatory controls and associated data strategies had failed to sufficiently mitigate the risks of systemic failure.

His response made it clear that he was not convinced that data and analytics were sufficient for mitigating the risks of future failures. He was adamant that both the United Kingdom and global authorities should provide credible explanations and rationale for the relevance of any new data or automation strategies.

"There can be little doubt that some of these asks would be inappropriate, unhelpful and unfit for purpose," Fred said as his frustration was starting to affect his typically calm demeanour. "Another concern is with the viability of some of these requests. The scale and volume of data we are talking about are sometimes absolutely staggering.

"How do you take the data of over 13 million customers, and that's just current account holders; how do you then take hundreds of millions of individual derivatives and turn that into something meaningful for the regulatory authorities?" Fred asked

> But there is likely to be an additional twist. If we are in effect unable to produce the right data in the right way to the right robustness, then that could actually send a message to the authorities that we have further barriers to resolution. This could potentially strengthen the authorities' view that more activities related to structuring the bank are needed.

He was alluding to a prevalent concern across the banking sector that central banks and their financial regulatory counterparts were convinced that one of the key changes that had to be made was a simplification of the structure of the world's largest banks. The thinking was that by forcing a restructuring along more historically traditional lines – where the high-street, retail and consumer banking parts were kept completely separate from investment banking or similar functions that were perceived to be more risky – would limit the risk of taxpayers having to prop up failing financial institutions.

> Perhaps we now live in an environment where we have to accept that as a requirement for building a successful bank – or part of building a successful bank – we have to make sure we can be successful in its resolution,

he said. "So going forward, we'll have to look both ways – we effectively have to consider both 'life' and 'life after death' – and that is difficult for a bank to do."

Though I did not disagree with Fred's assessment – that while data and analytics were important, they had previously failed to be the silver bullets for mitigating historical failures – I could not help but think that he was missing something much broader. I had no doubt that such a complex issue required a much more comprehensive perspective. I explained that I thought the bigger issue was not to do with the data or analytics existing in a single organisation or even within individual subordinate organisational business units – but that it was vitally important to consider the much broader implications of visibility and flow across the entire system. In some ways, this was analogous to the scientific findings about our brains: while each neuron is like the internal data stored within a single firm's system, it is the synapses, which form the bridges that facilitate the connections and flows between firms and the systems that lie within their internal boundaries. I wanted to help Fred see how the effectiveness of this interconnectivity was essential not only for the prosperity of individual organisations but for the integrity of the entire system.

> I think regardless of how much information is gathered, how accurate and timely it is, or how much insight can be gained from it, if it is all locked in silos, then we can have a situation where the entire organisation and even the entire system is effectively blind to such information,

I said.

We had been in conversation for over 45 minutes. We talked about many pertinent issues, with some focus on the triggers that had made organisations across the entire financial industry increasingly susceptible to falling victim to Lehman-like tragedies. It was evident that Fred was less than impressed with what he considered the knee-jerk reaction of regulators.

"What we need to realize is that the failure of banks is now on the agenda," he said.

> Rather than seeing it as an exception that might happen, it should now be looked at as something that can – and perhaps will – happen. And so, rather than focusing only on avoiding the inevitable, efforts should also be expanded to considering how we reduce the impacts of such failures whenever they happen.

This seemed a rather shocking admission, especially coming from a senior executive at one of the world's leading global banks – with a market capitalisation of over 20 billion dollars and total assets far exceeding the trillion-dollar mark.

What made this discussion even more intriguing was the prevalent perspective that there were some banks and financial institutions that regulators and central governments could not allow to fail. I had recently come across this controversy when I found myself caught in the crossfire between a financial regulatory team and a room full of senior banking executives.

The discussion was getting heated when the regulators pushed for a significant increase in data disclosures. They repeatedly stressed the need for the authorities to have more information – to be better prepared for an orderly resolution in the event of a future Lehman-like collapse.

A particularly passionate exchange happened between James, who led the regulatory team, and Sarah, a senior executive with over 25 years of experience with BBG's investment banking vertical.

"Look, this idea that some firms are in effect too big to fail has to be corrected," James declared. He went on to explain the regulatory position – that the taxpayer could not be expected to bail out insolvent firms without limits. And this was ample justification for the significant disclosure demands the regulators presented.

"I do not think this position is really tenable at this point," Sarah said.

> I don't know if I'm the only one who sees this, but we are in a very precarious situation with the global economy at the moment, and letting another Lehman happen now, where would that leave us? We have the U.K. in recession. We have a huge amount of debt across the Eurozone. We have a lack of growth in most of the Eurozone countries. We have austerity measures across the board. So, in my view, we are in it: we are already in a 'too big to fail' situation.

With great confidence, Sarah continued her rant – challenging the authority's strategy – for a few minutes. She was adamant that collecting more data – on the pretext that this would allow for an orderly resolution – was not a viable option. In her view, the economic outfall was going to be felt for another ten years at a minimum – and was inevitably going to look like another Japan with low rates and stagflation for a very long time. "We are well beyond 'too big to fail,'" she again asserted. "This is the new game now, and we are all in it."

The others in the room seemed taken aback by Sarah's open critique, but her viewpoints were not unfounded. Regulators across the globe have long stressed the importance of data for maintaining the health of financial institutions, with their thirst for disclosure increasing with every financial crisis or economic recession. The renowned American economist Frederic Mishkin took this even further by suggesting that "information failures" were potential contributors to the sorts of "credit booms" that ultimately lead to severe perturbation of entire global financial systems.

Beyond this, there was something particularly notable about the example of Japan Sarah had mentioned. Fuelled by cheap credit, low inflation and an abundance of innovation, the Japanese economic bubble of the 1980s led to a financial crisis of global and historical prominence. On record as a period of remarkable prosperity in Japan, with extremely low unemployment, relatively low interest rates, equity prices rising up to 600 per cent and land prices growing up to 400 per cent, the 1980s also ushered in a period now popularly referred to as "the lost generation." The effects of the crisis were purportedly exacerbated by the inability of the Bank of Japan to curb the excesses of national financial institutions insistent on providing credit to so-called "zombie firms." As organisations that had become extremely inefficient and contributed suboptimal productive outputs to the wider economy, "zombie firms" had only managed to stay afloat with unsustainable and conceivably artificial exogenous financial support, typically from national governments or financial institutions.

While Sarah's worries about implications similar to those witnessed in Japan were not implausible, most financial commentators insisted that analogies to a Japanese-style "lost generation" were exaggerations and extremely unlikely.

Yet my conversation with Fred, and his statement that we needed to shift the focus from the avoidance of a crash to the mitigation of its impacts, took on new meaning as I contemplated it within the context of the exchange between James and Sarah. What was particularly uncomfortable about both conversations was the number of unanswered questions – the gaps that felt unresolved by either the regulatory position or the measures that had initially been put forward by senior banking executives.

Even if banks and financial institutions across the globe would provide all the data regulators were keen to have, there wasn't enough evidence proving that this would indeed lead to increased stability and effective mitigation of future crises. While the strong conviction – that data could help to prevent debilitating damages to the system – seemed credible on the surface, the question was from where authorities had gained their confidence. Was it borne out of historical precedence or theories that had demonstrated that additional information was an effective way to mitigate such systemic risks? Has this approach previously been implemented or tested?

Yet while Sarah's position had landed like a bombshell, the response from the regulators was no less surprising.

"I do sense the challenge your comments portray, Sarah," said one of James' colleagues. "But since what we are asking for is data about the organisation and its activities, I must admit that I am really struggling to understand why such a request is being met with so much resistance."

It was as if an innocent question had undergone a mid-flight transformation that caused it to land as a piercing attack.

However, it seemed a logical inquiry. On the surface, all the authorities wanted was access to data that should already exist within the organisation, perhaps in increased quantity or with changes to scope, frequency and format. But if this was the case, why the reluctance to comply?

"That's a fair question," Sarah said after an awkward pause. Then she launched into an honest explanation that shed light on the mystery. She revealed that while the regulators' assumption was credible, there were internal challenges with implementing such changes in demand. Some of them would require technology updates that would consume considerable effort.

However, the main challenges did not come from an impossibility of the demands from regulators but were the result of organisational frictions, Sarah confessed.

> The most honest way to represent this is that our data, our teams and our systems are shaped in the way we currently run our business. And what you are asking us to do is to provide information that describes our activities in different ways. Satisfying such data requests would require flattening the firm's organisational silos all at once.

Sarah described how ways of working and capturing data – and the myriad of technologies for running the global business – had over the years become calcified in the shape and likeness of the organisation. Another executive, from across the table, interjected with additional concerns. They were convinced that such an ask – to flatten out the organisation's silos – would be incredibly challenging and lamented that such a programme of work would be unbearably costly.

They were right to be concerned about potentially significant costs, but I thought that there were even more significant challenges than those being called out. In my experience, such efforts to break down complex networks of siloed platforms, jurisdictionally distinct entities or disparate data repositories have historically not only led to very high costs and disproportionately low returns. In many cases, the shifts that such initiatives required were far too radical for the organisation to bear and, instead of delivering the desired benefits, often ended up inflicting damaging consequences.

Talk about costs was perhaps no secret but not every senior executive in the room appeared comfortable with the generous disclosure. However, the discomfort seemed to obscure a particularly important point: that the real challenge lay not solely with data but also concerned how individual silos across the organisation interacted.

Sarah seemed to have inadvertently hit the crux of the matter. Focus clearly needed to be shifted away from the silos – where data is captured, stored or processed – and more towards the synaptic bridges and tunnels required to ensure optimal transmission between one silo and another.

Yet I also considered whether further underlying concerns, forces that could stifle any chance of radical transformation could be at play at BBG. During my time within previous firms, I had encountered layers of fear that seemed innocuous on the surface but were capable of blocking forward movement. In those circumstances, proponents of change had been so focused on highlighting the benefits of a new situation that they missed addressing what might seem an irrational resistance to transformation. If this was the case for Sarah and other bankers, then the regulators had missed an opportunity to engage with such *concealed concerns*, I thought.

The potential of such hindrances to any data transformation was never far from my mind and the months that followed would go beyond confirming the existence of such *concealed concerns* across the firm and particularly highlight their prevalence across numerous industry sectors with regard to both data and organisational change.

Over the years, I have never been in doubt about the increasing importance of data. We already live in a world where our phone apps communicate with taxis, telling them exactly where we are, when we want them and where we need to be, a world where our smart TVs tell our providers what programmes we want to watch and when we would like to watch them, a world where our fridges and kettles – by passing messages through our smart meters – can tell our energy providers just how much power they are consuming and how much cash they are taking out of our pockets, and a world where communications between extraterrestrial satellites and driverless farm tractors are combined with open data to help decide when and where to plant seeds.

Yes, these crises had illustrated how far the impacts of things going wrong in the financial system reverberated across our daily lives. So, while a renewed emphasis on identifying tools for achieving more stability was understandable, I wondered whether data alone could really safeguard such a complex system? And if so, whether Sarah was right – that flattening firms' silos was the only sure route to meeting such increasingly sophisticated demands for organisational data?

Today, the answers are unmistakably evident. Over ten years after the crisis, the Financial Stability Board penned a paper to report on the progress that the G20 countries had made towards resolving their data gaps. Its findings were damning. In spite of this Group of Twenty intergovernmental forum comprising 19 of the world's largest economies and including the European Union (EU), in spite of the group collectively accounting for around 90 per cent of gross world product (GWP), about 80 per cent of international trade, up to two-thirds of the world's population, and roughly half the world's land area, it had collectively failed to resolve these gaps. The paper, in fact, goes on to suggest that such data gaps are becoming increasingly critical and can become exacerbated if a lack of data speed or information integrity hinders the potential for "market participants" to effectively identify, mitigate, contain or resolve the sort of pertinently systemic issues that seemed to increasingly affect us all.

The significance of these concerns drove me to reflect on a previous confidential conversation with James. There was little doubt that there was now more focus on data helping to drive action. I was particularly interested to know if there had been any precedence for where the approach of breaking down firms' silos had delivered the desired outcomes. I asked him if he was able to share some background information that could help me understand where the renewed confidence in the ability of this approach to help drive action in this way has come from.

I was keen to find out whether these strategies had been proven by either research or real-world application, and whether there were any lessons to be learned from previous implementations or established theories.

"Look, Ed, off the record," James replied.

We have to propose a data framework based on our experience of looking at firms we have had to resolve so far. We also have to borrow from the lived experiences of other global regulators. The problem is that we don't fully know yet. We are still learning what we really need from data and analytics and what the most effective approach to maximising their utilisation might be for banks and for other financial companies.

While his words didn't inspire certainty, there was something particularly raw and candid – perhaps even vulnerable – about his response. It may not have been the kind of straight answer that provided greater insight into the subliminal thoughts and considerations of rule-makers, but it left me in no doubt that regulators considered data and analytics as incredibly crucial for maintaining the health of the financial system and the health of the economy, not just for now but for the future.

James stressed that the regulatory approach was underpinned by a firm desire to work with firms to not only broaden and improve but also optimise and refine strategies going forward. He made it clear that the authorities were of the view that this was only the starting point of a deep and wide collaborative effort.

Part of our conversation touched on the current campaign for more data and more information as well as the strong opposition this elicited within the banking, insurance and broader financial sectors, as had been evident in the explosive conversation between the teams led by James and Sarah at BBG.

James thought part of the challenge came from some of the "fairly generic statements" used in preliminary papers that meant "to encourage the industry to think harder about certain issues." He suggested that these could have caused unintended levels of anxiety and agitation. More fundamentally, he expressed particular concern about the variety of ways banks and financial institutions were organised, which had implications on the complexity of monitoring and controls.

For a visual representation of the main challenge, I would choose the foundational triangle underpinning the core of a bank or financial institution. The three vertices would represent the following: one – the products and services delivering economic functions to their customers (such as cash deposit services, mortgages, credit cards or loans); two – the legal entities owning the underlying assets (such as buildings, cash machines or technology infrastructure); and three – the business units through which these assets are combined and managed (such as management structures and any variety of governance models).

At one end of the spectrum, some firms are primarily organised along the traditional legal entity lines, with such legal structures acting as unambiguous containers that encapsulate both their products and service offerings – and the business units with which such products and services are organised and distributed.

At the other end, firms employed a much more sophisticated business unit-led organisational framework.

But the majority of firms fell somewhere between these two extremes. Most firms organised their business along business units and, to some degree, across their legal entities. While this was a sensible way for firms to operate, it was incredibly complex from a regulatory oversight perspective – and even more so if a firm needed to be resolved in short order.

James, perhaps understandably, continued to justify the regulatory point of view, stressing that the authorities required the ability to view firms from different perspectives. He insisted that the suggested approach was important – and that firms now needed to provide very different sets of data.

While he recognised that firms were possibly struggling since this was not aligned with how they were organised, he seemed to miss something far more fundamental: a focus on the ultimate purpose, the "to what end."

There was no doubt that there was a requirement for deeper sets of data and for deeper insights but the ultimate purpose was to be able to unravel the underlying complexities that underpinned regulated firms. An extension to this overarching purpose was to find sufficient confidence that such insights could be reliably accessible on a regular basis.

This would suggest that, in order to meet this purpose, firms needed to provide the required insights alongside a clear accountability map to demonstrate that this relevant information could be assembled and delivered in a timely manner.

"Is what is initially required here, essentially, an effective and operational supersized data mapping exercise?" I asked.

"Absolutely," James confirmed.

> But we understand that this will take time. We need to have realistic expectations and accept that changes don't happen overnight. But we also need to make it clear that just because financial institutions previously made data available in a certain way, there is no guarantee that this is what we are currently looking for.

James's statement – that having made data available "in a certain way is no guarantee" this will meet future requirements – which seemed a direct response to Sarah's earlier disclosure, seemed fair. Yet, while there could be little doubt that firms would benefit from structures that were sufficiently flexible so that interactions between constituent parts could be adapted, a focus on this objective seemed misplaced and counterproductive given the stated ultimate purpose.

In other words, rather than the challenge being limited to data insights – there was an attempt to extend it beyond this "to what end" and towards how individual silos across an organisation interacted.

Yet a few things were less opaque. It would have been naive at best – or downright dishonest – to downplay the emerging tensions between firms and their overseers. Everyone seemed to feel a heightened level of vulnerability that stemmed from pairing an uncertain situation with the desperation to act. It was also clear that, from the regulatory perspective, there was firm determination that something had to be done. And data had been named the antidote for addressing the challenge.

As I reflected on our exchange, two things became clear. Firstly, data and analytics have suddenly assumed an incredibly critical role across the business and economic landscape. This is both scary and exhilarating. Data might not be the new oil powering industry or the new oxygen that mankind needs to breathe, but data has become pivotal for maintaining global stability at a scale never experienced before. However, it is also obvious that the strategy and thinking lack the depth and breadth required to both address underlying challenges and take advantage of significant opportunities that are increasingly emerging. While the increased relevance for data and analytics is ambitious, there remains an unmistakable fear that even such a paradigm shift could prove insufficiently bold to enable the grand vision of mitigating the risk of future financial meltdowns.

An additional matter that remained unclear was why James had been so reluctant to be drawn into the "too big to fail" versus "too small to save" debate. For me, this left some question marks, especially since this had been one of the triggers for the most recent and passionate debates between regulators and the firms they oversee.

2

Too Small to Save?

Coming back from a quick run on a cold and wet autumnal morning, I was surprised to see my phone's display light up. The message simply asked, "Can you talk?" In addition to the economical word choice and unusual timing so early in the day, I was particularly intrigued to learn that it came from Richard, who had never sent a text nor reached out via my private number.

I had known Richard, one of the most respected insolvency professionals, for years. He did the kind of work where people would imagine a team of 12, all dressed in black trench coats, arriving at the door on the day a company slips into failure.

But Richard was nothing like that. Instead, he had dedicated most of the last three decades to working with large multinational organisations to try to avoid such occurrences and plan for the best possible mitigation should an organisation be left with no choice but to fold or cease trading. He had risen quickly through the ranks and was now one of the foremost experts to make partner at his firm, one of the biggest accounting and professional services networks in the world, with over 300,000 employees worldwide and a revenue base of over 40 billion dollars.

Puzzled by the cryptic text message, I decided to give him a quick ring back. I knew that I wouldn't have a chance to speak to him later due to a schedule packed with back-to-back appointments.

Richard picked up right away. "Good morning, mate," he said. "Sorry to contact you so early but I'm having a meeting in a couple of hours and wanted to get your opinion."

He explained that he was due to sit down with the executive leadership team at BBG. Having heard about the increasingly hostile atmosphere that was emerging due, in part, to age-old disagreements about the role of data,

DOI: 10.1201/9781003278276-3

he was certain this topic would come up. He was keen to gain some additional context and test some hypotheses.

I confirmed that this had indeed been the case but there was something particularly strange that I wanted to highlight. I had found that rather than confront the key challenges surrounding how data might be able to help and how to enable action to address any impediments along the way, there seemed to be those who were keen to shift focus to other matters.

I described a recent meeting I had attended. I was expecting a conversation focused on new data sources that were being touted as essential for addressing key financial risks, "but, to my surprise, the focus was suddenly redirected towards the contentious subject of 'too big to fail,'" I said.

"I am not terribly surprised, if I'm honest," Richard said.

> I suppose this all comes from what some of the key players are trying to achieve with the information they are looking for. So, if you think back to pre-crisis times, a lot of the data that was being provided would have been around monitoring the capital position of the bank.

Indeed, before the financial crisis, focus had predominantly been on understanding the future business plans of banks and financial institutions. The main objectives were to determine to what extent capital requirements were being satisfied – and data disclosure demands primarily revolved around the key financial metrics required for such assessments.

The challenge with that approach was that it was mainly backwards-looking – focused on how firms had performed historically – which was great for describing what had transpired in the past. It was, however, particularly lacking for such key questions as "how can early warning signals for future chaos be identified to enable effective course correction?"

It was the kind of standard challenge habitually directed at financial statements: that they are predominantly focused on historical – and not at future – performance. Now, it was clear that mindsets were shifting. Information that had been adequate for enabling ongoing monitoring and supervision of banking activities was no longer deemed sufficient. The authorities wanted more.

It soon became clear that what the authorities wanted was not so different from what organisations are increasingly trying to achieve and what societies around the world increasingly need. Today, in a world where the chances of catastrophic failures are on the decline but where the impact of such failures is often disproportionately severe, sophisticated techniques that can detect and prevent these anomalies are urgently needed.

Organisations are collecting more and more data, with originating sources going beyond humans to sensors and devices of various forms. At the same time, firms are increasingly driven to strive towards hyper-targeting and hyper-personalisation. This dichotomy requires more and more effective means of separating signals from the multitudes of data points that companies are now having to wade through.

The implications of this challenge are also increasingly felt in our individual daily lives. The exponential rise in the level of sophistication we now live within means that we are experiencing significant increases in both the costs and the impacts of any disruption to our daily lives. Losing a mobile phone may, on the surface, seem quite trivial but such a situation could prove not only costly but significantly discomforting. The relatively rare occurrence of a leak induced flooding of our home may not only be incredibly inconvenient but could lead to irreplaceable or unredeemable loss.

In spite of health and longevity being on the upward trend within the most developed global economies, a focus on separating signal from noise is becoming absolutely essential. This is perhaps most easily evident with the proliferation of wearables and health related mobile phone apps, which churn out significant volumes of data and which provide vital inputs for some of the kinds of anomaly detection algorithms that are increasingly becoming of critical importance to our life experiences.

More broadly, there has never been more demand for applying data science to effectively separate significant signals from the endless barrage of noise we are incessantly being subjected to.

As this trend becomes increasingly prevalent across organisations and societies, and as we continue to see the relationship between the occurrence and the magnitude of loss become increasingly inverse, making data work will become even more vital – not only for enhancing our experience but also, most fundamentally, for enabling our existence.

The increasing susceptibility of the financial sector to the kind of damage that such relatively small anomalies can inflict on comparatively large systems is reflective of this much broader trend, across industry sectors and across society. Richard referenced the work we had kicked off on the recovery and resolution planning (RRP) for banks and financial institutions. "So, this new regime of RRP is effectively trying to do something incredibly different," he said. "It is all more operational, more forward-looking, more scenario-driven – and it is all driven by the fact that these banks could fail."

"That's interesting," I said. "And that is effectively the link back to regulators stepping away from the traditional idea that some banks were 'too big to fail'?"

"Precisely," he confirmed. Previously, information requirements were based on the assumption that large banks could not possibly fail, but recent events showed that planning for such eventuality was often incredibly lacking.

"Perhaps the interesting thing, Ed, is that until recently, history seemed to have effectively validated traditional approaches, because such failures hardly ever happened," he said.

There was no doubt that this statement was factually correct. Yet, this mindset was even more of an indication of the dangers that potentially lurked ahead. It was precisely these kinds of infrequently occurring but significantly impactful events that required careful attention. These were the sorts of signals that required early identification and the kinds of anomalies that could lead to devastating effects.

Yet, there was no shortage of those who have traditionally stood in the way of the kinds of transformations that would allow data to sufficiently underpin such changes in focus. Among them was a trio of senior executives within the U.S.-based investment and capital vertical of BBG, who were informally referred to as the New Yorker Terriers. Rumour had it that the two women and one man making up the group had earned this nickname because their oscillating – and often unpredictable – behaviour mirrored traits associated with the breed of terriers. On the surface, they seemed as considerate and cooperative as a friendly dog wagging its tail – but they had a reputation for switching to more combative and aggressive positions to fulfil their secretive agendas, much like terriers are reputed to growl and then bite, as soon as you turn your back.

In our conversation, Richard and I recalled a particularly unpleasant incident with the trio. It had begun days before a crucial working group session, which I had convened within the first few weeks after I had been brought in as a strategic adviser and to help deliver a critical data programme. We had crafted a draft strategy paper alongside a participatory contribution plan for individual representatives from all verticals and strategic business units across the globe. Days before the conference, the PowerPoint slides were shared with the most influential stakeholders. A walk-through meeting with one of the trio had started off with some apprehension since some of the strategy's recommendations for addressing bottlenecks meant a change to the legacy approach for the capture and distribution of derivative data sourced from the investment banking division. To my surprise, this apprehension quickly eased, giving way to what seemed an unlikely alignment. By the end of the meeting, I had the impression that the team had done well to present a sufficiently compelling case, and the trio was finally onboard.

However, the events of the next few days were to disperse this sense of accomplishment. While the 90-minute global working group meeting started well, it did not take long before some of the hard-won pre-meeting pacts came crashing down. It was brutal. Rather than achieving the reduction of barriers as sought by regulators, the meeting progressively accumulated new barriers between internal functions, partly enabled by blatant denials of positions previously agreed to by the New Yorker Terriers.

"How on earth did that just happen?" One of my team members asked, giving voice to our perplexity after the meeting. There were a number of hypotheses on offer, but the most likely was that these politically engineered obstructions had been masterfully crafted to protect existing power bases and to ensure no legacy controls were conceded.

I later contemplated that we might have overlooked the vital signs of something even deeper. I wondered about potential parallels to the situation that led to Sarah's crossfire with the regulators. Could this cloak of obstructions be the result of deep-seated underlying issues? Was this yet another example of a missed opportunity to engage with *concealed concerns*?

Regardless of any potential underlying motives, one thing was obvious – there was significant resistance towards the proposed strategies designed to provide the supervisory authorities with confidence in BBG's ability to deliver frictionless data across all its globally dispersed verticals.

Whilst their underlying motivations might indeed have been significantly different, it was particularly striking to observe similarities between misgivings that I had previously identified with James' position and the position we were now being confronted with by the New Yorker trio. Their actions were unlikely to deliver outcomes aligned to the ultimate purpose or the ultimate "to what end."

Whilst his view that firms were possibly struggling because it was requiring firms to transform into ways that they have not been organised, his thoughts seemed to miss something far more fundamental: a focus on the ultimate purpose and the ultimate "to what end."

As I listened to Richard's assured voice over the phone that morning, I felt sure that no amount of political manoeuvring would shift his perspective on the current situation. He was increasingly convinced that the current crisis had forced the hands of authorities – and that the traditional control tools that central banks and other rule-setting institutions had pulled over the years were no longer sufficient. He also made it clear that there was now a renewed call for dismantling organisational silos due to their reputation for impeding the use of data and analytics for increasing economic stability.

While the approach sounded familiar, there were fundamental differences. In stark contrast to the strategies of old, Richard suggested that regulators were now trying to apply data and analytics for answering very different kinds of questions. They were posing questions like: how do you predict the point of a bank's potential failure, how do you plan an effective recovery and, if necessary, how do you resolve a bank efficiently?

This shift meant that authorities were redirecting their attention from a singular focus on financial metrics towards far more emphasis on foundational structures. Yet, there were even more questions that had to be answered, such as "how is the bank structured? And what are its actual economic functions?"

For a bank, key economic functions typically include issuing money to customers either through a vast distribution of automated teller machines (ATMs) or over the counter in often extensive branch networks. Among a broad variety of other economic functions, banks are essential for credit intermediation and are particularly effective in the role of middleman between savers and borrowers. They are also critical for the provision of credit products, such as credit cards, mortgages and personal loans.

The idea of shifting focus towards key economic functions is becoming foundational in the minds of global rule-makers. This thinking seems to have emerged out of the experience of overseeing only a limited number of firm failures.

The origin of this mindset shift is unmistakably correlated with the story of the failure of Northern Rock, the Newcastle upon Tyne-based bank. After only recently boasting a 75-window branch network with over 5 billion dollars in revenue, it became the first British bank to fail in 150 years, due to a bank run. Formerly a building society, Northern Rock had demutualised in the late 1990s, and, during the early 2000s, became heavily exposed by overleveraging to fund an ambitious foray into the mortgage market.

The exercise of resolving Northern Rock at the point of its demise – including data analysis performed by the insolvency practitioners – led to the realisation that not all functions of a financial firm were vitally important to the broader financial system.

Data makes clear that, while some activities are very profitable and provide very helpful services, a lot of the services provided by financial organisations could be lived without. However, analysis showed that there were some things people could not sustainably live without: for example, an effectively functioning payment system. Without a functioning payment system, our ability to buy or sell goods or services would be severely hampered.

Yet, the essential element in this interaction – between goods or services and firms or their customers – is enabled by a financial system which is underpinned by the exchange of data.

An even more fundamental understanding of how the system is made up enables a much deeper insight into both its brilliance and its fragility.

> I think the reason why we developed this idea of critical economic functions was to look at firms slightly differently – and that's one of the reasons that data has become so critical. In effect, we need to work out what bits of the firm are important and what bits are less important at points of intense stress or at points when a firm becomes insolvent,

Richard explained. "So, this new drive is meant to ensure that we all focus our efforts on collecting the right data for the important bits and spend less time on the less important bits."

It is fair to observe that this particular flavour of categorisation is relatively new and had not been applied before – certainly not on this scale. It requires a significant level of data analysis to enable it to go into a far lower level of detail – and much beyond any levels of in the past. It requires data at a level of granularity similar to that required for the kind of hyper-targeting and hyper-personalisation drive that organisations across all sectors are increasingly desperate to achieve. On the one hand, there could be no doubt of the benefits that such a level of data acquisition and creative exploitation of available data could deliver – both in terms of direct commercial benefits and underlying risks mitigation. On the other hand, it is clear that achieving this is going to continue to require fundamental shifts in how banking and financial firms are run.

I found Richard's explanation particularly insightful. In effect, he seemed to allude to the increasingly popular hypothesis that the information that currently flowed in and out of firms and across the financial system was inadequate for sufficiently understanding what went on within individual firms and what the key signals for systemic stresses were, as well as any key associative triggers or early warning signs. This situation was exacerbated as the size, reach and complexity of the financial system – and its underlying institutions – increased.

However, in order to try to obtain more relevant information from firms, the authorities had identified – and created a separation between – what is critical and what is not. The real challenge was that historically, such economic functions had no direct linkages to the individual legal structures within banks. Legal structures, such as legal entities, were the preferred unit of engagement for rule-makers and supervisory authorities, who saw them as appropriate containers for essential items like contracts, transactions, liabilities and protections, which relate to a firm and how it is run.

I like to think of each legal entity as an individual silo that needs to interact with other silos. With the construct of legal entities, market players can easily understand what relationships exist within a market and what interactions are in play. However, things are often more complex in the real world. Organisations have multiple legal entities grouped under a single umbrella. BBG, for example, behind the scenes owned over 2,000 legal entities at the time of the recession – and could actively engage in trades or other market interaction with any number of these. It was also incredibly challenging to inextricably link a single economic function to a single legal entity – and vice versa, making it more difficult to unravel the complexity of interactions both within organisations and across the entire financial system.

For me, it was intriguing to see how some of the views expressed by the authorities were being corroborated by Richard.

Yet, Richard went even further. He stressed that the level of information his banking clients were now compelled to provide by regulators was to enable a critical function contingency analysis. While this novel analysis regime was originally crafted to help the authorities formulate a much better understanding of the economic functions that were most critical to societies and to economies at large, I would later find that its applicability was far broader than for the financial sector. In my experience across several industry sectors, I found that its fundamental approach provides very helpful tools for utilising data to understand the distinction between those aspects of the firm which act to deliver direct revenue returns and those that are essential for "keeping the lights on"; a kind of distinction sometimes referred to as attack versus defence.

On the surface, such analysis seemed just another increase in demands by regulators. After all, it wasn't the first time there had been such a sweeping change. Every new set of regulation appeared to require either new data points, new data formats, new data transfer mandates, new data frequencies or any combination of these. But this time, it was not just about content, structure, frequencies or formats.

"The vast majority of the additional information being requested is all about how to better understand scenarios. It is all scenario-driven," Richard said.

> This is an important distinction between the legacy mindset and the current thinking. To be honest, I have been in this business for donkey years now, and these sorts of things weren't even in the regulatory lexicon before these crises

While his explanation made sense, I couldn't help but think that it didn't address the kinds of technology barriers exposed by Sarah or the kinds of people and culture barriers that some influential players like the New Yorker Terriers were likely to create. Without a fundamental shift in the way people and technology were organised, this regulatory ambition of a financial system made resilient through the creative utility of frictionless data was unlikely to come to fruition. Without the wholesale dismantling of long-established and progressively calcified cultures that underpinned most silos, it was difficult to imagine how the level of information flow envisioned by the authorities was likely to materialise.

Richard seemed more optimistic. Regulators across the globe were under so much pressure from their individual central governments – and this would force the exertion of significant coercive muscle over the firms within their supervisory orbits, he felt. And this would ultimately compel executives of financial institutions to drive the radical transformation of their organisations.

"I think the crisis has changed the game," he said. "The regulator is now asking two fundamentally different questions – and is trying to achieve two fundamentally different things." Initially, information was required to identify the gaps and frictions within the system, help mitigate any issues found and help prevent the kinds of frictions that can lead to failure. "It is really about understanding what options are available to a firm to actually stop it from going further down the road of failure and then leading to systemic failure," Richard said. However, should this be unavoidable, then data would be required to help take the actions necessary for safeguarding the broader system and for avoiding economic catastrophes.

"There are, in effect, two levels," Richard explained.

> You see, the thing about this new data is that it can act as a trigger for recovery and resolution but it can also act as a facilitator of recovery and resolution. So, we can look at data from those two very distinctly different standpoints.

"Interesting," I mused. It was clearly quite a novel way for financial authorities to think of data. Similar to the Covid-19 pandemic, this was yet another indication of how failure being on the agenda drove the need for authorities to do all they can to maintain the financial stability of the economy. This is driven by the need to ensure that you and I can go to an ATM and know that we can withdraw our wages or savings whenever we choose – and that we can confidently go into a shop and pay for our groceries without fear of our cheques or cards not working. It really is as fundamental as that.

Whilst this view of data for the purpose of protecting us as individuals and for reducing risks to organisations was essential, I could not help but think that it was substantially one-sided. It seemed to fail to engage with the other beneficial outcomes that data and the advanced analytics that it enables can provide: such as enhancing organisational outcomes and for delivering improvements to our individual ways of life.

Richard went on to say that this new focus was "going down the path of 'can a bank save itself from failure?' and if it can't, then how can we ensure an orderly resolution in order to protect the rest of the system?" This brought us back to the controversial "too big to fail" debate. Richard seemed to be alluding to an emerging policy to allow large firms to fail if they became so stressed that they would struggle to continue operations without sizable public fund injections.

"Are you suggesting that the era where large firms such as General Motors and AIG were bailed out to avoid failure was effectively over?" I wanted to know.

"Absolutely. So, we must now have the right tools in place to make sure this has as limited an impact on the system as possible."

Much before and much after this conversation, data-focused financial regulations have continued flooding in. Perhaps most notable amongst these would be wider packages that are significantly underpinned by data, including the United States' enactment of Dodd-Frank and further evolutions of the European-originated Basel Accord. Closer to home, a publication by the U.K.'s Financial Services Authority stated that "the benefits of increased financial stability to taxpayers, the financial sector and the wider economy from the collection of information" through its new regulatory instrument called "recovery and resolution plan" were "likely to be considerable."

Yet there were also credible voices casting doubts on our ability to legislate our way to resolving silos across the financial system and to enabling the kind of frictionless data flows that such legislative frameworks depend on for their success.

One of these voices belonged to the widely acclaimed economic historian and Harvard professor, Niall Ferguson. In his BBC Reith Lecture on the Darwinian Economy, he argued that historical precedence indicated that such proposals could have the opposite effect to what was intended. Ferguson insisted that the regulatory environment is plagued with multitudinous complexities that act to hinder its effectiveness, including political motivations and conflicts of interest. Exposing the potential for conflicts of interest, careful analysis of the professor's thoughts presented a significant dilemma for the authorities: that they are dependent on the firms that they regulate for the information required in order to regulate firms. Controversially, he also claimed that "excessively complex regulation" could indeed be the "disease of which it purports to be the cure."

Beyond this, there was also concern that these new data regimes appear to be overly focused on the state of singular entities – as opposed to the health of the entire system. This approach seems even more concerning given its skewed attention on the largest organisations.

"So, what would happen if a small organisation providing a critical service to the rest of the system was suddenly at risk," voices of concern wanted to know.

Were we finding ourselves in a world where some firms were "too big to fail" while others were increasingly at risk of being "too small to survive"? There was also the conundrum of "too important to fail" versus "too large to rescue," which seemed to underpin some of the thinking leading to the Dodd-Frank act. The events of the coronavirus crises have made clearer than ever that lots of small firms are much "too important to fail," relegating to the abyss any historical notions that might have alluded otherwise.

Just as were the authorities, Richard was absolutely right to highlight the importance of this distinction between – between critical and non-critical functions of organisations. It is also difficult to dispute the organisational distinction between the big and the small. Yet, it is clear that these viewpoints miss an important point: much as small things aggregate up to make big things, big firms and large systems are often underpinned by much smaller units and far smaller entities. And so, I was of the firm view that a lack of focus on these microelements of the broader landscape, which are often considered silos, would be a significant oversight and one that is likely to be detrimental to the ultimate purpose.

Perhaps just as significantly, a strong financial system not only requires sound entities but also requires viable and resilient interconnections both within and between its individual parts. This raised concerns that a focus on individual organisational silos was likely to be much too narrow. It was increasingly clear that making data work needs a significant shift in historical strategies and in the approaches of old.

Richard seemed attuned to these concerns. He admitted that regardless of such regulations, unravelling large financial institutions had historically proved to be a difficult process.

"This has been proven with previous situations such as the Lehman Brothers' failure," he said. "There are huge challenges with it."

As an insolvency practitioner, he saw the need for a silo-free frictionless environment to ensure that information is consistently accessible and fully up to date.

> So, at any point in time, you want to be able to have an accurate cut of the balance sheet, sliced and diced by any one of the myriad possible dimensions one might need to look at. The data should be sufficiently flexible to be organised by legal entity, by economic function, by product or service lines, by business units, or any combination of these,

Richard said. "But it could also be by jurisdictional impact: either from a source or a target perspective."

He added that he would need to have accurate and timely data about all the staff, all the properties, all the IT systems and all contracts. "But it's a moving beast – as you know – and that is why the flow of data needs to be boundless," he said. "This is why data needs to be flexible and adaptable, especially considering the sort of size and complexity of some of these institutions."

I found this conversation to be just as energising as the morning run I had just returned from, but a quick glance at my watch suggested it was time to take stock and bring matters to a close.

I wanted to highlight two key insights that I wanted Richard to take away from our conversation. Firstly, there was no doubt that global economies are increasingly inherently unstable, partly because they are underpinned by an inherently unstable financial system and partly because of the speed of change that we are continuing to see in the world around us, and partly because they are fundamentally underpinned by an increasingly complex interconnection of incoherent silos. Secondly, it was clear that data and analytics were increasingly becoming central tools for stabilising our unstable economies.

Richard agreed.

> But, I must add this, Ed. I do absolutely agree with this drive for data and analytics. I have no doubt that this will help facilitate a more stable outcome for BBG, other financial firms, the entire financial system and the global economy. It is that big a deal. But, coming back to the previous point, until you actually unpick the silos and the frictions that make the entire system so difficult to unravel, and until we are able to address the inertia and the rigidity that makes organisations far too slow to adapt, collecting more and more data can only go so far. It is a key step. It is an important step – and it will help – but it will not be the silver bullet.

Richard's statement sounded like a dismal surmisal of a hopeless situation. There clearly were lots of unanswered questions, most pertinently, "How on earth were we to begin to unpick these silos?" And, "how do we start to address the inertia and the rigidity both within and across organisations?"

Realising how fast time had sped by and that I had mostly listened rather than lent support for Richard's upcoming meeting, I said, "I must apologize, Richard, I didn't mean to hijack so much of the call but I was really keen to hear your views."

"No, this was very useful," he said. "Helpful as always to bounce off ideas with you, especially where data and analytics are key ingredients. That is precisely what I needed."

After exchanging pleasantries, we ended the call.

3

The Disclosure Conundrum

The pub was fairly busy for a weekday evening. Most booths and stools were occupied with a lively drinks-after-work crowd, and the pints seemed to be flowing far too freely. From the din, I could just about make out some snippets of conversation that revolved around the topic of the day: Dunfermline – the century-old building society that was once the largest in Scotland and among the top 20 in the United Kingdom based on total assets – had ceased trading. The news of this latest in the string of global bank failures seemed to inspire a palpable nervousness with people wondering which organisation might be the next casualty – and what that might mean for their livelihoods.

This seemed a fitting setting for the conversation I was hoping to have with Sarah about her piercing remarks in that memorable meeting two months ago. It was the first opportunity to have an open informal conversation – and we managed to find a spot where we could just about hear ourselves speak.

As the waitress walked away with our orders, Sarah turned towards me and smiled, "So, I suspect you would like us to start with my explosion the other day?"

There was no shortage of controversial viewpoints – about the economy, about the future of the financial sector or even about the role of data in an increasingly complex and interconnected world. However, as I recalled her passionate argument with the regulatory team, I couldn't help but think that there was more to her uncharacteristic outburst and encouraged her to elaborate.

"You know I am not one to lose my cool, and especially not in a professional situation. I could have ended up with an HR incident," she said with a laugh. The outburst had alarmed her sufficiently that she had immediately jumped on a call to express her sincere apology for her demeanour.

DOI: 10.1201/9781003278276-4

She had also proactively sought advice from internal employees' well-being resources.

Soon after our drinks order arrived, I wanted to dive straight in to satisfy my curiosity. "We know that banks and financial institutions already insist that they are completely inundated with requests for data from the regulatory authorities in fulfilment of various requirements," I said.

"Yes! Constantly," she interrupted, her irritation noticeable. "But there is a renewed emphasis on it these days – on even more information disclosure."

A recent statement by the U.K.'s Financial Services Authority (informally called the FSA) had outlined that the authorities needed even more information to enable them to resolve big institutions in an orderly fashion should resolution become necessary. I was keen to learn Sarah's thoughts about what these perceived data gaps were and how helpful such additional information might prove.

"What you find is that the FSA does come to us quite a lot, especially during times of stress," she replied without enthusiasm.

> Effectively, the first thing they want to know is, 'What is your exposure? What are your positions and your exposure to various different countries?' Especially when there is any kind of blow up in another bank or country or anything in the news.

Concerns about a potential Eurozone crisis were rife at the time, and authorities across the European continent were keen to get ahead of the game. Significant attention was being focused on gaining clarity on the aggregate risk exposures of individual banks and financial institutions, especially in countries deemed unstable. Regular analyses and reports providing information on such balance sheet risks were required to include breakdowns like derivatives, "market to market," primary exposure and bond-holding positions. This was intended to ensure that the rule-setting authorities were sufficiently capable of building predictive models of potential future outcomes and predetermine the most suitable interventions.

The key problem statement here was an assessment of organisational resilience. It was intended to answer such questions as, "if one of a firm's key markets were to fail, how could the firm demonstrate its ability to work out how it is going to be impacted." On the surface, this was about organisational risks: to provide some modelled analysis about situations such as, how much a firm is likely going to lose or how much such an issue could hurt its capital base. However, considered more deeply, this was much broader: it was not only about potential impacts to an organisational silo but also about the wider implications across an entire system.

Sarah went on to describe what was being touted as the potential for several countries to exit from the European Union. While some of these countries had been members of both the Eurozone single market and its customs union for decades, some had recently come up against severe financial difficulties and were at significant risk of national defaults. An additional complication was that some of these countries were also members of the Eurozone's Monetary Union (EMU). This meant that any such exit would also have implications for the EMU common currency: the Euro.

> What they desperately want to understand is, 'OK, if one of these countries goes down – for instance, for us, a Greece default could mean a haircut of 75 percent – what actual impact does that have to the rest of Europe compared to the kinds of crises we have dealt with in the past?

Sarah explained with a level of concern that suggested she thought this unlikely scenario was actually becoming possible.

"So, what's the key concern you were trying to raise – that you consider regulatory priorities somewhat misplaced?" I wanted to confirm.

"Yes, but that's not the full picture," she said.

> What I am seeing is that the way things are these days, everything is systemically entwined. That's my real concern. This is why I am absolutely convinced that there isn't such a thing as letting a big bank or small bank – or a big country or small country – fail without serious knock-on effects.

This response was unexpected. Rather than a rallying cry against potentially excessive or misplaced demands for data, Sarah's main concern was with the suggestion that financial institutions – big or small – could be left to fail. Aside from the implications this might have for depositors and account holders of individual banks subject to an insolvency-induced crash, she seemed particularly concerned about the broader ramification for the entire system. Her focus was on the increasingly complex interconnectedness both within and between actors and players across the financial landscape. Beyond the linkages enabling money transfers from one bank account to another – via a complex web of movements – these connections also governed the communications and broader interactions between financial firms operating within the financial system.

We both agreed that data was key for helping to gauge potential knock-on effects of a specific shock to the system. Due to the scale and complexity of the entire system, a strategy limited to descriptive analytics-driven data-exposure reporting would improve such a situation and significantly reduce current blind spots, I explained. But in isolation, it would be inadequate for determining the broader implications of a single failure on an entire system, regardless of whether the failed unit was big or small. In line with this reasoning, I proposed that focus must shift from a "what happened" descriptive analysis to an even deeper "what if" scenario modelling. While such analytic approaches have very wide applicability across use cases and across sectors, it should in this instance be capable of exploring questions like,

> What would happen if a member state like the U.K., Italy, Poland or Hungary was to leave the European Union? What would happen if the entire Eurozone was to break up? What would happen if a country like Greece was to leave the EMU? What would happen if there was a sudden and complete disaggregation of the Euro currency?

So, rather than looking backwards – and producing data analysis revealing individual sector performance – it was pertinent to consider the potential implications – the "what if" – of something happening in the future.

"So, the current situation must compel you to project and provide information on how certain scenarios might play out?" I asked.

"Yes and, in reality, this is a very difficult thing to do because no one really knows," Sarah said. "There is no mechanism for a Euro breakup and there is no mechanism for a country to leave the European Union because that was never envisaged when they put everything together."

We talked about the role of data science and analytics for modelling such scenarios, and how, due to a lack of comparable historical precedence, there had only been limited "war gaming" to comprehensively mimic a number of potential outcomes. And since legal frameworks were so effectively employed for the integration of such complex entities – rather than their orderly disintegration – some analysts feared that, without much deeper use of data, both firms and regulators could be left with no alternatives but to guess what might happen.

"Imagine for a moment that a significant event, like the collapse of the Euro or the failure of Greece, actually did happen," Sarah said. "Can you imagine the myriad of implications, the number of combinations and permutations? It would be an absolute disaster."

Indeed, this was not an easy set of circumstances to contemplate. It would mean the sudden collapse of structures that had been taken for granted for half a century – structures that underpinned our financial and economic systems and that were deeply embedded in our everyday lives.

I considered this in light of the work we had kicked off a number of months ago, trying to make sense of BBG's over 100,000 globally dispersed employees, thousands of properties, hundreds of technology platforms, scores of jurisdictions and 2,000-odd legal entities – all positioned under the umbrella of a single global brand. A key ambition of this global effort was to collate data sufficient to trace and map the parent entity's complex internal interconnections – in effect capturing all the relationships that were vital to our internal processes.

I wondered whether this maze of an internal system we had been trying to unravel was analogous to the broader economic and financial system within which it was embedded. Could the understanding of the interactions within and between internal silos serve as a helpful precursor to disentangling the systemic interrelations that define global economic and financial exchanges?

We think of silos as internal data systems, computers, technology applications, teams, departments or even individuals who predominantly act in isolation. Could we consider an organisation to be a silo if it acts in much the same way – within the context of the broader system within which it interacts? What if the organisation predominantly acts in isolation or if its data, computer systems, teams or people are suboptimally connected to those of other organisations within its network and within its scope of interactions?

As Sarah and I considered these questions, we decided that the analogies converged – and that there were at least two sides to the information that the authorities were keen to capture.

"Are they asking, 'What are the complexities that exist within your organisation? What are the interconnectivities? What are the interrelationships?'" I asked. "And if we understand that better, then we could also leverage data and analytics to perhaps understand what might happen if things suddenly go crazy."

"Exactly, that is what they are trying to gauge. Whether that's possible or not – this comes down to opinion," she said. "Some would argue that it would be a desperately difficult thing to do, but I wonder how the regulators would respond if we put this question directly to them."

"And I suppose there is one of their head offices just up the road," she added jokingly in reference to the FSA buildings only a few minutes' walk from where we were sitting.

Her comment was laced with the kind of sarcasm I have often come across over the years when stakeholders assume data aspirations had crossed the imaginary chasm between "never been done before" and simply "impossible." Yet, time and time again, such presumptions have been disproven.

There is no doubt that resolving data complexities to identify the most helpful signals that lie at their points of intersections is anything but trivial. Yet, like many senior leaders, I feared that Sarah might have been somewhat blindsided by the debilitations stemming from the mayhem. To me, the prize was much bigger and broader than satisfying regulatory requirements or even guaranteeing the survival of the financial system, important as they were. To me, the prize was a win-win outcome, which included the valuable insights that such a resolution would bring.

I could see such insights helping to transform the financial firms that were able to look beyond ticking the compliance box by revolutionising the way their offerings interacted with their customers. I could see businesses transform from being reactive to being proactive, from just responding at times of distress to being able to predict and possibly prevent situations of distress from occurring. I could envision them redefining relationships with customers, who could choose to become active partners rather than passive payers for services.

I found that the implications even went beyond the banking sector. For instance, in my experience with the chemical industry, finding such intersections are leading to the much faster delivery of more profitable yet safer products. In insurance, we are starting to see these intersections enabling timing interventions that are reducing the risks of fatalities: improving human experience while reducing the implications of large losses and significant claims. Perhaps most pertinently, we are seeing the identification of meaningful interconnections leading to accelerated research and positive outcomes, at scale, within the healthcare sector.

Although Sarah's comments were focused on the perceived risks of systemic disruptions to the banking sector, they raised important points with broad implications.

I recounted some of my conversations with senior rule-makers, including the suggestion that it was the regulators' ambition to use data differently – to not just better understand organisations as a "going concern" (which was the historical viewpoint) but from the perspective of how their associated legal entities enabled the specific critical economic functions they delivered to society.

Their views suggested that the new approach to information mapping was influenced by public opinion regarding the government's handling of financial crises. In my conversations, several officials had been unequivocal about the view that no organisation should be "too big to fail."

"When firms are called 'too big to fail,' my question is, 'Why? What is it about them that is 'too big to fail'?" one of them insisted. "No firm in itself is that systemically important. Instead, it's the activities the firm does that can be systemically important, but the firm is just a shell."

It was their view that the activities firms engaged in and the services they delivered needed to be looked at separately. They argued that working closely with firms – and analysing the data at a much more granular level compared to the pre-crisis regime – would enable a richer understanding of the individual services that are of particular significance to the broader economy. Such an approach would make it possible to distinguish highly critical from less critical functions and allow more focus on the functions that are deemed essential for the smooth functioning of the entire financial system.

This was a radical shift from the way the authorities had previously analysed banks. It meant that rather than considering the viability of an entire bank, like a Santander or an HSBC, the authorities would instead ask questions like whether HSBC's mortgage service is critical to the entire financial system. Or whether the sudden discontinuation of Santander's credit card service would have a debilitating impact on the system as a whole. If the answer was yes, then these services may be categorised as critical economic functions – and the organisation providing them may be classified as a significantly important financial institution (or SIFI).

It was also a radical change from how banks and financial institutions had previously viewed themselves. A categorisation of significance, as determined within the four walls of the organisation, was typically bestowed on services that delivered commercial benefits to the firm. And these often depended on shared service functions – such as technology or call-centre operations – within a business.

It was clear that this discrepancy – between the functions that were internally commercially critical and those of critical importance to the broader economy – posed a key challenge for capturing data at that level of detail: data required to better understand not only individual services but their internal and external intersection points, data needed for identifying barriers for potential resolution as well as preparing firms to have the right information available should it become necessary to actually undertake a resolution.

There was little doubt that the ultimate goal was to be able to allow such "too big to fail" firms to fall into administration as should be the case in an effective free market, just as they would in other industry sectors. Yet, the Lehman Brothers case had demonstrated how difficult it was to resolve such firms without good data and without good analysis.

As I related these sentiments to Sarah, she interjected, "But it really is too late for that stance. We have already put ourselves in a position where organisations are too big to fail. Take the clock back 20 years, and it wasn't like that."

She was adamant that the world had undergone a supercharged acceleration in the meantime, becoming more vulnerable as a result.

"Everybody is trying to get a slice of the pie! And that means financial products have become more and more complex, and balance sheets have become more and more leveraged and intertwined," Sarah insisted. "So, you are now at a point of no return. You are beyond 'too big to fail.' It's a new game now."

It was a startling position – contrary to that of the rule-makers – yet Sarah had an important point. At a time of so much instability and uncertainty, the political priority of most European and Western governments was to "batten down the hatches, protect themselves in readiness for turbulent times, and stabilise things before moving on," she insisted.

This was undoubtedly an interesting perspective. It was fair to suggest that the regulators had learnt lessons from the Lehman Brothers and had accepted that significant data gaps had presented a challenge for resolving the situation. Efforts to gain an understanding of what happened with the organisation had been hindered by a lack of both availability and integrity of information at the point of the crisis.

I told Sarah what a regulator had once admitted to me in confidence. "Firms have provided data to help us identify significant legal entities," he'd said. "And that has been crucial as we try to get our heads around these very large organisations."

She replied,

> There was a gap because we were in a world of 'light-touch' regulation. The
> Treasury department decided that we didn't want full-on regulation as it

hindered a bank's ability to grow – it hindered the country's ability to grow. With 'light-touch' regulation, there were bound to be gaps. But the game has changed now.

Sarah insisted that the gaps of old had hurriedly been addressed and that "everyone now knows what everyone's got."

If that was true, it would mean that the challenge of silos – the barriers introducing friction into interactions across the financial system, a situation amplified by the Lehman Brothers crash and which regulators had been grappling with for ages – was speedily being resolved.

Could Sarah be right? Could there be light at the end of the tunnel? And if this was beginning to work across banking and finance, could this model be applied to other industries and organisations grappling with the deep-seated challenge of silos and ineffective interactions?

"So, everyone is better disclosed now," she emphasised. "But isn't that just as bad?"

Rather than pausing for a response, Sarah continued to argue that in a financial system underpinned by fully disclosed markets, banks would likely be unwilling to lend to each other – since the balance sheets of most banks are often unappealing.

"You are almost better off being in a situation where you don't know what is on everyone else's balance sheet," she said. "So you have free flow of funds, and market liquidity is maintained."

Positioning silo-busting over-disclosure against silo-building under-disclosure, as Sarah presented, had all the hallmarks of a divisive argument, yet this was not without precedence. The current-day political economies of the world's wealthiest nations are inundated with clamours for financial-stability-enhancing regulation. Such regulations are typically built on an ideology that sees robust and timely availability of information as ready remedies for all ailments of the financial system. The Dodd-Frank Act is one example. Responding to widespread calls for changes in how the financial services industry is overseen, the act underpinned President Barack Obama's proposal for a "sweeping overhaul of the United States' financial regulatory system," for which he envisioned "a transformation on a scale not seen since the reforms that followed the Great Depression." In addition to a raft of changes to the financial regulatory and oversight establishment across the United States, this single act enshrined in law regulatory requirements for the provision of over 20 new data sets and analytical reports.

However, there is no shortage of experts who are diametrically opposed to a race towards extreme disclosure. For instance, an influential write-up on *The Transparency of the Banking System and the Efficiency of Information-Based Bank Runs* suggested that enhancement in the dissemination of information, as is intrinsic for the efficient application of the kind of market discipline compelled by the Dodd-Frank Act, could be counter-productive. The *Journal of Financial Intermediation* publication, which investigated "the relationship between the transparency of banks and the fragility of the banking system," insisted that exposing too much data to customers or other market participants could actually spook recipients and incentivise undesirable actions, such as mass withdrawals, bank runs or banks deciding not to lend money to each other. This reflects the belief that the extreme flattening of the silos – which serve to create boundaries between financial firms on one end of the spectrum and their customers and other market participants on the other – could lead to unintended consequences. The article also stated that the timing of information flows can have either stabilising or destabilising implications for the financial system. Although this view goes against the grain of the position of mainstream policymakers, these suggestions should not be overlooked. After all, the two authors, Iftekhar Hasan and Yehning Chen, are internationally renowned professors of finance.

Some other financial experts have voiced similar concerns. The respected economics and private enterprise professor David Vanhoose, for example, proposed that information disclosure by financial institutions could indeed increase the likelihood of "bank runs," which could lead to systemic failure. Meticulous analysis of this supposition revealed that the situation described was primarily concerned with banks already in distress, yet the argument also raised serious concerns about the implications of the level of transparency that could result from the eradication of silos.

The portrayal of information as a double-edged sword, which these opposing viewpoints seem to propose, could leave us with the impression of incompatible – even paradoxical – propositions for the appropriate future of organisational silos and a befuddling dilemma for data utility maximisation strategies.

In one regard Sarah was absolutely right: there was a twist. On the one hand, regulators felt compelled to propose that having more information would be beneficial for potentially highlighting areas of concern and telling us more about how a difficult situation might be resolved. Yet on the other hand, bringing more information into the open could serve to raise potential concerns and stifle the flow of funds – in effect creating the problem it was fashioned to solve.

"The problem is that there are too many problems," Sarah continued.

> If you had the U.K., Cyprus or Greece as isolated incidents, for example – or if you had one organisation in distress and everything else was booming – then that might be fine. But you have many major governments in Europe so heavily indebted that they need to implement significant austerity measures and cut their deficit. And they can't do that because everyone is rioting, and this means everything becomes politically entwined as well.

She believed that the over-abundance of issues across both regional and global financial markets – with all banks complicit to some level or other – made it unlikely that data disclosure would be the easy fix so desperately desired.

"It might have been alright having full data disclosure if only a small number of companies had a problem," she explained.

> Then I could say, 'I know BNP Paribas has a bit of a problem, so perhaps there is a billion dollars' worth of exposure to be concerned about.' Yet, we could live with that because our balance sheet is massive and we have plenty of liquidity allowing us to carry on. But since there are far too many in such precarious situations, not even our balance sheet could possibly cope if they all came crashing down at the same time.

Sarah's views were different from those held by mainstream commentators, yet her insights seemed to leave me with more questions than answers. They did not, for instance, help me better understand where things went wrong with the Lehman Brothers and other "too big to fail"-type institutions. When I pressed Sarah for her thoughts on how organisational silos and the data disclosure conundrum might have impacted the current crisis, her response was no less assured.

"I do not agree that Lehman's should have taken everyone by surprise the way it did," she said.

> You only needed to have looked at their business model, look at the data and their balance sheet. Their model was much the same as Northern Rock's. They had no depositors and were completely reliant on other banks and other institutions for funds. Such funds could have been cut off tomorrow. And that is precisely what the market belatedly chose to do: cut off their supply of liquidity, so they were suddenly left with no cash flow and no money to continue trading.

Banks that relied on a decent amount of market liquidity and the ability to borrow from other financial firms for their survival would continue to be exposed to severe risks, regardless of the proposed new frictionless and silo-free data disclosure regime, Sarah stressed. In fact, she was convinced that increased disclosure would only serve to increase such risks.

Until banks could deleverage to a point where they're able to operate without the interbank funding market, they would always be extremely susceptible to heightened risks of market reactions, Sarah explained.

> But then, this would not be a market, this would not be banking, this would not be finance. Then we would be going back to the 1920s, when a bank only lent money when it had the money, when a bank's liquidity came from its deposit base. However, we now have this massive animal that is driving us forward and gives us no choice but to rely on each other to keep the system going.

Throughout our conversation, Sarah maintained that she didn't see the new drive for data disclosure as a viable solution for addressing the market's ailments, even if extreme disclosure enabled greater understanding of the complexities and interrelationships both within and between firms.

I, on the other hand, found it difficult to accept that a situation where information flows were boundless and organisational silos demolished would be devoid of positive outcomes. This view was also shared by a number of credible experts, including Bob Diamond, the high-profile CEO of Barclays Group. He had recently offered his entire organisation as a test case for the new data-led recovery and resolution plan regime – in a move that industry commentators considered to be a clear demonstration of his confidence in this approach. The press was also curious about his rationale for taking such a bold step. Was this a real show of trust in this new role for data? Was it based on the belief that age-old silos could be upended, that analytics could live up to our expectations and deliver the answers, that extreme information transparency could unlock markets and ensure stability? Or was this a potentially calamitous political stunt?

When I posed these questions to Sarah, her answers may have come back quicker than expected – but they were no less thoughtful.

"Well, what are the alternatives?" she said.

> The issue is, what can you do to either retain or gain back that confidence in the market? What can you do? The only thing you can do is to be as transparent as possible – and hope that the confidence will come back. And

hope that this would lead to the ability of everyone to trade with each other, and lead to the opening up of struggling financial markets.

Her comments were by no means directly supportive of the new role for data, but they did point at something fundamental: the role of confidence for ensuring market stability and the role of boundless data transparency for enhancing confidence. Sarah was inadvertently suggesting that more transparency could lead to an increase in the level of confidence in the market and that such confidence could – in itself – improve market liquidity and underpin financial stability.

There is no doubt that amidst Sarah's frustrations, she was on the right path. Considered much more broadly, smoothly functioning businesses and their interactions across their chosen markets are either enhanced or encumbered by one important intangible: confidence.

Yet I couldn't help but think that Sarah might be missing something of particular relevance: trust. Throughout my experience, it has become increasingly clear that transparency – by itself – is insufficient for driving confidence. When data is transparently exposed but lacking in integrity, it consistently fails to improve confidence – often leading to the exact opposite situation.

Put differently, my experience across various industry sectors has shown that rather than hinging on the quantity of disclosure, trust is more closely correlated with how data can be made available and its perceived intrinsic credibility.

So many years after the start of the crises, it is intriguing to see that one of the fiercest debates continues to revolve around the quantity of disclosure, even today. While there is consensus that the current level of disclosure is inadequate, many are concerned that by shifting into what some describe as "information overdrive," we could end up with the other extreme. This perspective is indirectly supported by the mindset that underpins increasingly stringent data protection regulations, which are firmly anchored towards the under-disclosure end of the spectrum.

Could we end up with unintended negative consequences, not only across financial markets but across retail, hospitality, health and other sectors of the economy, if too much is disclosed?

There can be little doubt that there are inherent risks associated with over-disclosure, just as experience has shown that a market plagued with the ills of under-disclosure is unsustainable. Instead of the never-ending antagonism by arguments anchored at either end of the spectrum, the ideal situation is to find the appropriate intersection between these two extremes.

As desirable as a balanced situation is, the big question – of whether this is actually achievable – remains. And if the answer is yes, then how could we begin to navigate the gulf that separates the legacy of under-disclosure from proposals that could lead to over-disclosure? And how can we begin to find the appropriate intersection between these opposing positions?

In the world prior to the crises, these considerations did not seem to matter at all – yet in the world that followed, they are all that seem to matter.

Part II

In the Heat of Frustration

A Deep Dive into the Implications of Organisation-Wide Data Obstacles

4

Harnessing the Power of Frustration

I remember it well. It was about 3:30 a.m. on a Saturday morning when my phone rang. Startled awake, I picked up to find myself confronted with a nightmare situation.

First, I was informed that an entire critical service stream at TAG, one of the largest multinational financial organisations in the world where I worked as head of data, was down and had caused a failure in the process that updates the central motor insurance database relied upon by law enforcement agencies. Shock very quickly turned to horror when I realised that customers who had recently bought car insurance policies from us had been detained by the police – due to our service failure, police officers had found no record of valid insurance policies in the central database for the cars they were driving.

The nightmare continued when investigations revealed that our organisational silos were at the root of the mayhem. A failure to share vital information across the 24/7 support teams had rendered them powerless to avoid this catastrophe.

It became clear that addressing silos had to be our top priority, but this in itself presented a problem: the ambition to break down organisational silos was not new and had long been at the top of our list of priorities. How had this item eluded all efforts of turning it from rhetoric into action?

Only a few days before the wake-up call and not long after I had joined this firm, I had found myself in a very heated meeting in a full and crowded room. The atmosphere could not have been described as pleasant, but much of the obvious acrimony was understandable, since some stakeholders had been waiting to get their hands on their data requirements for frustratingly long periods of time.

As I left the room, I was accosted by Albert, a rather unhappy senior data scientist, who made it clear that he could not understand why there were so

DOI: 10.1201/9781003278276-6

many hurdles to jump, why the simple seemed so hard and why we had to have so many data silos even within the walls of our own organisation.

"Do you know that this is the first company I have ever worked for where the business teams seem to be so far ahead of the technology departments?" he asked. While he didn't expect a response, I had to concur and agree that he had a point.

Such frustration was not uncommon in those days and the extent of the disgruntlement had become obvious within weeks of taking the leadership mantle at TAG. There was no shortage of dissatisfaction with the outputs of the data department and the sense of discontent, which seemed intrinsically associated with data, seemed to be voiced at every opportunity.

In fact, only a few days before my discussion with Albert, I had been summoned to the office of one of the most senior executives of the entire group. She was extremely frustrated because she had been waiting over five years for the organisation's data to yield tangible results to satisfy some of her most critical requirements. While I initially assumed that her reference to "five years" was an exaggeration, my team later confirmed that an associated data product request was actually issued 1,951 days prior to our conversation. She also had serious concerns about the operational performance of some existing data and analytics products, including one that sometimes took over three weeks to deliver tangible insights.

It was clear that the data supply chain was broken. At the time, it consisted of a collection of several insufficiently engaged parts – a system resembling an incongruous assembly of inharmonious components. In addition, the technology supply chain was also fragmented. It had evolved into a landscape of incompatible platforms forced together through an unlucky combination of organic growth and incongruent acquisitions.

Beyond these, many of the channels intended for the facilitation of cross-organisational communications were also broken.

While these failings were often attributed to the spaghetti-like infrastructure that resulted from speedy and sometimes incomplete integrations of networks and desktop tools, closer investigation revealed that the organisation could benefit from strategies to enhance the integration of the many diverse cultures coming together from various originating backgrounds and organisations.

Yet beyond all this, team members widely shared the ambitious vision of taking the organisation through a journey of radical transformation that would enable it to adapt to meeting the needs of customers today and in the future.

For instance, this vision included shifting car insurance from the current model of "mobility insuring" to one of "mobility securing" – daring to imagine a situation where a customer has an accident. Rather than having to call about the insurance and getting stuck in a seemingly endless loop of "your call is important to us," the insurer is automatically notified via telematic data transmission from an in-car black box device. Imagine if this would trigger the rapid deployment of required services, such as a drone to take photographs and enable claims assessment, a tow truck or recovery vehicle to deal with the car and an Uber to take customers to their desired destination if they don't need medical attention. Imagine a service that goes even further – to enable helpful interventions before lives get disrupted. One where intelligent use of data helps to identify points where a driver's behaviour or observed environmental conditions might indicate heightened risks of an accident occurring and incentivise appropriate pre-emptive action. In the example of insurance, such risk prediction and prevention scenarios could apply to virtually all types of coverage. Every one of these interactions would be powered by artificial intelligence, robotic automation, machine learning, the internet of things or blockchain. And, every interaction would have to be enabled by data – which needs to flow seamlessly through multiple pipelines and processes across entire value chains.

Such a world seemed incredibly distant, from where we were at TAG, as I sat with my cup of lukewarm instant coffee and listened to Albert's concerns. As he expressed his thoughts, I was reminded of a recent experience during my time consulting on a large programme at a European multilateral organisation, where the impacts of silos led to devastating effects.

It was no easy day to forget. It was no less than minus 17 degrees Celsius on a cold winter's morning. A look through the conference room window revealed a park covered in a thick blanket of snow and pedestrians braving the biting cold, leaving behind trails of the frosty breaths they exhaled. Inside, the volcanic heating system seemed to be struggling to dispel a decidedly frosty atmosphere coming not only from the frigid outdoors but also the aftermath of a critical deadline that had recently been missed. The international press had made a meal of it – and the tension felt tangible as well as intense and uncomfortable. The inquisition – and finger-pointing – were in full swing.

Where had it all gone wrong? We had been well aware of the deadline, and the risks of missing it had been highlighted over six months before the new publication was due to go online. Work streams were split between disparate teams and across multiple location silos, but communication frameworks had been effective in the earlier parts of the project. It was true that locations were distributed across countries, but there had been limited resistance and lots of flexibility shown by third-party teams, including an openness for travelling as much as was required. When a blockage caused delays to third-party contract approvals, the challenge seemed to be self-imposed – there was no budget shortfall and funding could have been reasonably easily secured.

So, how could we have found ourselves in such an uncomfortable situation, where walls had unnecessarily been built around teams that desperately needed to interact? How could the design and integrity of the entire system be validated when data flows and team interactions were so severely hampered by the imposition of restrictions that now seemed misplaced and unhelpful? It seemed incredibly illogical, but in hindsight, it became clear that we had become our greatest enemies.

As I considered the analogies between the two situations – the missed opportunities, the lack of inter-team communications, the implications of silos and knock-on effects across the entire community – I contemplated sharing the experience with Albert, but the timing did not seem apt. His focus was exclusively on the here and now. After all, the more recent organisational circumstances were arguably unique – and my experiences were not only from a different company but also from a distinctly dissimilar organisational sector.

Albert told me that his entire team was stuck, although fault lay not with the team members. Their frustrations regarding data availability and access had become a familiar theme. Yet, they weren't the only ones who were frustrated. There was no shortage of stakeholders with concerns about the challenges with linking data sets from multiple sources, especially since standards were wildly different and definitions were inconsistent. There were also complaints about the amount of time and effort it took to validate data inputs and their associated outputs. Quality was varied – even within individual sources – and opening up channels of communication between teams to increase the chance of getting such challenges addressed was perhaps even more difficult than accessing the data systems for which the teams were accountable.

Albert was particularly concerned about a perceived inflexibility stemming from the silos that dominated the organisation's data landscape. A further reason for his concern was the sense that even when interactions were achieved and value delivered, there was a distinct lack of adaptability, especially since such interactions had a tendency to be quite rigidly defined. He lamented that the organisation did not seem to cope well with rapid change and struggled to transform as use cases and demands varied, evolved or became more complex over time.

Deeply concerning as his thoughts and comments of this particular challenge were, I couldn't help but think of some big stories – clearly in somewhat different contexts – that illustrated the broader impacts of silos.

I recalled the famous failure of the European space agency, and how this uncomfortable catastrophe was attributed to a strategy where individual countries produced different parts of the rockets. Analysis suggests that the explosion of the rocket – assembled from independently sound parts – was actually caused by poor inter-team collaboration. Yet while Europe struggled to come to terms with the blow-up of the $600 million Ariane 5 within 96 seconds of its maiden flight – there was much better news across the pond. In the United States, NASA, which had historically struggled with disconnected silos and endured failures of its own, moved to avoid such a painful recurrence by bringing its third-party suppliers in-house and by ensuring that every individual contributor understood the entire project.

Another big story that flashed through my mind was General Stanley McChrystal's *Team of Teams* depiction of the U.S. army's initial challenge in Iraq – of fighting an Al Qaeda that moved faster, regrouped quicker and adapted at pace. The military, however, solved this by implementing a radical shift away from the traditional "siloed" command and control structure where significant pieces of the data jigsaw were either classified or "need to know" – to an approach where individuals were effectively networked and where weekly live meetings were held with the entire task force to enable unfettered visibility into leaders' thought processes. These safe spaces also encouraged and empowered active contributions from every individual among the intentionally assembled cross-functional group, enabling effective execution and rapid operational adaptability.

Albert, in the meantime, expected me to play a pivotal role in addressing our organisation's conundrum.

"You are the head of data with ultimate CDO accountability," he said. "So why can't you just break down all these needless silos?"

While it may have been tempting to douse such fiery exasperation with a deluge of defensiveness, I found it beneficial to just let it all land. In order to truly appreciate his position, I had to try and sit in the pain and frustration with him. Perhaps this would also allow me to get a grasp on some of the underlying concerns?

After all, previous experiences suggested that there might be *concealed concerns* hidden behind Albert's cloak of frustration.

Not very long after this encounter, I noticed some relevant headlines in my daily news feed. Lemonade – an InsurTech company powered by artificial intelligence, behavioural economics and the financial backing of one of our rivals – announced that it had set a world record for the speed and ease of paying an insurance claim: three seconds and zero paperwork.

My mind immediately went to our recent conversation. *What would Albert think now*, I wondered as I imagined the additional frustration this news might bring. Such results could only come from the kind of "silo free" operation where a seamless flow of data and unencumbered team interactions were the norm.

For me, talking about these scenarios was especially frustrating since I knew them to be possible. After all, I had worked in organisations that functioned the way Albert described: where organisational hierarchies didn't hinder engagement and interactional frictions were extremely low. I had also experienced strategies that helped a number of organisations along their transformation journeys towards achieving such desirable outcomes.

Albert was painfully aware that we had recently lost some key resources to competing organisations. It was also no secret that we faced serious challenges attracting top talent. While his was not the only department impacted by this, Albert's team had been especially exposed to such risks because it included individuals with particularly niche data science and analytics competences.

"Some people seem to be open to taking a pay cut elsewhere just for the possibility of gaining excitement," he lamented.

Of course, Albert was right to see a connection between my role as head of data and his aspiration for a "silo free" organisation. Such views were shared broadly across most of the corporate world. In fact, it was extremely rare to have two or more executives in a room and not have the issue of silos come up. Beyond that, the vision of breaking them down was a common feature in organisational strategy ambitions and never far from the lips of those whose interactions had been sufficiently hampered by the frictions typically attributed to silos.

Yet it was obvious that despite considerable efforts dedicated to neutralising this perceived barrier, positive resolutions seemed in embarrassingly short supply.

Was it time to radically rethink our approach?

Or were silos a nemesis you and I – and the organisations we work for – needed to accept? Does this require a shift in focus towards strategies for some sort of mutually acceptable coexistence instead or would any attempts at fixing this age-old challenge be no more fruitful than the futile exertions of the past?

When Albert took me aside after that particularly heated meeting, our conversation went well beyond the typical five-minute rant. It very quickly started to feel like a "meeting after the meeting" rather than a quick debrief. Despite being on the receiving end of some uncompromisingly delivered grievances, I was keen to take advantage of any opportunities for the kind of open and candid exchange that the power of frustration sometimes presents. In addition, this was a rare and welcome situation where such spontaneity was unencumbered by a diary blocked with back-to-back meetings.

As he was sharing his frustration that his team members were spending over 90 per cent of their time addressing the consequences of the silos that caused blockages across their intended lines of interaction, I spotted an opportunity to switch gears: I was keen to gain his perspective of what "good" actually looked like. With a shift away from the idea of silos and towards what we were actually looking to achieve, the conversation gradually transformed into a productive encounter – one pointing to the identification and implementation of potential solutions. Perhaps even more insightful was the fact that by making the transition from fears and concerns towards purpose and "to what end," we were able to find a path towards resolution.

As the conversation progressed, it became increasingly clear that the outcomes Albert envisioned had nothing to do with – nor depended on – the breaking down of silos. His key concerns revolved around the need for speed. He longed for the sort of flexibility that would allow his team to iteratively experiment and rapidly unlock opportunities for delivering value for the organisation. He also envisioned a level of adaptability that would enhance our ability to expediently react to changes in market conditions or the competitive landscape.

"I just do not understand why we should have to struggle to connect to anything or anyone within our own organisational boundaries," said Albert, suggesting that even on the rare occasions when his team managed to bring things together, they were often exposed to the kinds of overheads that come with a muddled, disjointed and incredibly fragmented data pipeline.

As he began to delve into more detail and I scribbled away on my notepad, I couldn't help thinking that it was unlikely that I would have felt differently in his shoes.

I realised that in order to build robust data foundations for data science and artificial intelligence, a paradigm shift was clearly required – towards a world where interactions were seamless, change was quick, and adaptability allowed for feedback to be rapidly absorbed to enhance outcomes.

While I was pleased that switching gears had led to this shift in focus towards resolution and that we had arrived at this point of clarity, I was again reminded of the similarity between this situation and previous experiences. A standout example was a conversation I had with a senior insolvency practitioner during the recent financial crisis. Like Albert, he was in no doubt about the significance of data and analytics for solving organisational challenges. He even accepted the premise that data and analytics could help facilitate stability for the entire financial system and the global economy. However, he was quick to point out that addressing the silos – and the frictions that made the entire system so difficult to unravel – were absolutely key to achieving such an ambition.

Yet for me, breaking down silos didn't seem the logical conclusion. Instead, it felt like the kind of ambition that had led to many failures over the years, the kind that had generated much frustration, born out of a realisation that such a goal was improbable at best and had often ended up being counterproductive.

Insights gained from examining the cause that led to the system's failure at TAG – and the fateful early morning call – would ultimately allow me to find a more credible approach for dealing with the silo conundrum in a fashion that would lead to the delivery of tangible productive outcomes.

5

Why Did It All Go Wrong?

Looking back at the nightmare incident that resulted in the unwelcome wake-up call on that Saturday morning, I recalled the initial panic. While some were concerned about the implications for customer experience, others were immediately alarmed about the potential implications for the firm's image as a global brand.

"What if the press got wind of this?" some worried. "What if some of the customers wanted to sell the story?"

"Can you imagine the headlines?" a concerned colleague asked.

In the hours and minutes in the immediate aftermath, minds were as focused and actions as swift as possible. But soon, attention was redirected internally – to probe the origins of the issue.

Even at the time of the call, my thoughts had immediately gone to Jo, one of the subject matter experts for the service that had failed that night. He had taken a lot of the blame – not only for the issues that led to the service failure but also for the lack of sharing of vital information with the 24/7 teams. Having access to this information would have significantly increased their ability to avoid or reduce the impact of the event.

Yet, I was convinced that Jo wasn't incompetent. As someone with over 20 years of experience in data and analytics, he knew the technology platforms inside out. Even more broadly, he was very knowledgeable about the organisation to which he had been dedicated and loyal over many years. He saw his colleagues as an extension of his family and often worked late hours without being prompted to do so.

So, why had Jo been at the centre of this incident? How had he allowed such a critical system to become so fragile? How had he become not only a single point of dependency and a single point of failure but, in effect, had also become an individual information silo?

DOI: 10.1201/9781003278276-7

These were some of the pertinent questions we attempted to answer, yet my direct leadership team went further – turning its attention towards the underlying root causes of this dire situation. One senior team member of the team, who was convinced that there was nothing sinister about Jo's actions, helped to expose aspects of the organisation's culture that he felt were at least partly to blame for the event.

So, where were the gaps? It was true that Jo had a rich technical background and deep understanding of our systems, but this knowledge had not been sufficiently shared. He had never gone out of his way to explain, "Here is how this thing works. Here is how it all hangs together, and here are a few pitfalls to be aware of."

Yet this wasn't due to a lack of social skills. Jo was a water cooler attention grabber. He never held back on his opinions about everything from football to politics, yet this well ran dry when it came to sharing his abundance of technical knowledge with team members.

"I cannot believe that hoarding of vital information can be anything but sinister," said a colleague who had been impacted by the mishap. "It's not exactly as if he is some sort of introvert, recluse or socially inept."

Another said, "He is just selfish and only cares about making himself indispensable."

As I continued to explore the situation with my senior team, we discovered foundational challenges that went far beyond the responsibility of just one team member, like Jo. Some of our technology infrastructures could benefit from an update and much of our software was dated and cumbersome to use. Some of our code bases were unwieldy and difficult to manage.

Yet, less tangible challenges also came to light, and these seemed to cause the most significant concerns.

"Have you heard the rumours about the secret black book?" one colleague asked, referring to a practice attributed to a feared and powerful senior executive. "I was told that the names appearing in there never make it onto a promotion's shortlist, regardless of how well they may perform."

Disclosures began to reveal a history of blame and finger-pointing. The stories that were being exposed suggested a deeply entrenched culture where things turned ugly when something went wrong, with its extreme manifestations only evident in times of crisis. In the immediate aftermaths of failure, there would be an inquest under the guise of a "root cause analysis," or an RCA, as they were frequently referred to. On the surface, RCAs were meant to unearth the lessons that can be gained from difficult experiences. In reality, they were considered witch hunts – a means to deduce who was at fault and who was complicit in what had gone wrong, and a source of data for the dreaded "black book."

There could be little doubt that such an environment would have implications on how individuals chose to behave and interact.

Yet, some of my team members thought Jo had reacted with a heightened sense of accountability and ownership, which seemed to suggest a kind of boldness one might associate with an environment where people felt safe to take initiative. Others thought he came across as unashamedly coy, tight-lipped and secretive – just when openness mattered most. How could such incompatible sets of assessments be reconciled?

One of Jo's closest confidants later revealed that beneath that appearance of boldness lurked something so deeply concealed. They revealed that a deep-seated anxiety and a fear of failure drove Jo to get things done himself and not only shy away from any in-depth review of his work but actively obstruct such efforts. This vicious cycle culminated in a situation where Jo became the single team member on whose knowledge the service depended – and thus the ultimate single point of failure.

However, the same confidant suggested that Jo had a deep sense of commitment to the organisation and to its customers. Despite the crisis, many colleagues never doubted Jo's integrity. Further exploration revealed that he had received multiple "individual star" rewards as part of an internal system aimed at providing recognition of collegial appreciation.

The evidence of the crisis incident illustrated a significant misalignment between how individual team members on one hand – and the firm on the other – perceived the creation of value. I would later find that this was not an uncommon challenge.

We also found that a culture of blaming, as was illustrated by the rumours of the "black book," contributed to these kinds of insular and secretive attitudes, and they were not confined only to Jo. I wondered if things could have been different if he'd been given an opportunity to safely speak about – and address – his worries.

This reminded me of situations I had previously encountered, where opportunities to affect change had been missed because such fears had not been confronted. Would this become yet another missed opportunity for engaging with concerns that had been concealed?

Our work in the days and weeks that followed revealed that Jo's predicament was no isolated case – there seemed an endemic culture of individual silos across teams.

Another example came from Lancelot, a data engineer with extremely specialised and sought-after expertise in a niche platform called Kalido. His skills and knowledge, gained over decades, were not only in short supply among TAG's ranks but across the industry more broadly. A long-standing failure to build capacity in this area of expertise across the firm led to significant bottlenecks that posed critical operational risks, especially since the platform was deeply embedded in our technology landscape.

Yet another expert and a data architect, Uduje, had evolved a custom-made internal reporting system that had become critical to parts of the business. When he threatened to leave (shortly before my arrival), the firm offered him a lucrative non-standard financial package to avoid risks to this valuable system. He accepted.

These were not the only areas where data architects were potentially capable of holding entire business processes to ransom due to their essential knowledge about how particular parts of the systems functioned.

While it would have been easy to jump to the conclusion that such behaviours were driven by individual self-interest, a number of incidents suggested that something deeper was amiss.

Our technology infrastructure was undeniably fragile and susceptible to failure. Yet, beyond the disruptions directly caused by such undesirable events, the heightened chance of failure also triggered a set of unintended consequences: opportunities for an underlying finger-pointing culture to bubble to the surface.

Every additional interview, meeting and conversation scheduled to further the investigation revealed that it wasn't the actual failures that most people were preoccupied with. Instead, they were worried about these unintended consequences.

This powerful insight resonated with my previous experience of working with teams and people across industry sectors and large multinational organisations.

The findings suggested that experiences, and especially what happens when things don't go according to plan, count more than any organisational rhetoric the likes of, "You are empowered. You can try new things. Let's learn from failure," of which there was no shortage at TAG.

How people are treated when things go wrong determines – at least to a certain degree – whether they feel confident to be open about their work and about suggesting changes to the way things were done or to their culture. Clearly, in the battle between rhetoric and intentional leadership, there could only be one winner.

In fact, experience suggested that two of the most important opportunities for real and tangible change happen around points of failure: one just before failure happens and the other in its immediate aftermath.

At this point, it had become obvious that the wake-up call could serve as a trigger for urgently required organisational change – to address the two key challenges underlying otherwise unique situations: insufficiently connected silos and significant value misalignments.

I momentarily cast my mind back to my latest interactions with Albert and his reaction to the news headline about Lemonade, the InsurTech company that had secured a world record for the fastest claim's payment on the planet. It had jolted the realisation of how far away we were from delivering customer experiences even remotely close to this. We worked in an environment where many individuals felt disempowered and restrained, where big talk about "thinking outside the box" never seemed to lead anywhere, where information silos were the norm, and where interactions were severely hampered by unhelpful frictions.

I was more and more convinced that our ordeal with silos did not only present serious challenges for interactions between one department and another, one team and another, even one functional area and another – but also affected interactions between individuals within these departments, teams and functional areas. And implications went far beyond the superficial, the rhetoric of senior executives or the glossy displays of PowerPoint presentations. Not only had we felt the brunt of a highly distressing disruption to our customers' lives, but the status quo also came with undesirable consequences for our organisational growth and hampered our ability to adapt to the fast-evolving battleground for competitive advantage.

And so, a clearer image of the challenge had emerged. We had to eliminate the silos that impeded beneficial interactions across the firm, that limited our ability to fully leverage our rich data assets and that pushed us far behind in the race towards implementing cutting-edge solutions, such as with data science and artificial intelligence. And above all, silos were posing a risk to our ability to deliver on our highest priority – of putting our customers first.

While the challenge was right in front of us, the path to its resolution was not as obvious. Could an age-old traditional approach deliver success? Could a focus on people deliver the desired outcomes, perhaps through measures like restructuring teams, forming working groups or mandating steering committees? Such efforts had been tried countless times, not just by ourselves but in other firms across industry sectors – yet there was little evidence to demonstrate their ability to eliminate the interactional frictions silos bring. Could an approach focused on technology present a more promising way to get there, perhaps with new tools and techniques, such as DevOps or microservices architecture? Again, none of these ingredients seemed to add up to becoming a secret sauce, since similar ideas had been tried and failed to deliver these required outcomes.

The next big question was, what now? Why had none of the traditional approaches been successful in solving the silo conundrum? Were silos a kind of nemesis you and I – and the organisations we work for – just needed to accept? Was this a lost cause or should we shift our focus towards strategies for some sort of mutually acceptable coexistence – where the benefits of silos can be observed without any inherently undesirable consequences?

There is no denying that the results of my earliest efforts to break down our silos weren't any different from other countless attempts.

Yet due to the recent incident, there was progressive alignment with a vision that changes to the ways we worked – and our legacy technology infrastructure – needed to happen. However, realising such goals didn't seem any closer, and my initial attempts were met with firm and unyielding resistance.

I remember contemplating the two circles of change that would be required: one, with the inner circle of data analytics practitioners and two, the outer circle across the broader firm.

"Even if we could successfully break down the silos within the data circle, how on earth are we ever going to be able to dismantle the silos across the broader organisation?" I thought to myself. It seemed an undertaking that was destined to fail; yet another initiative with an exuberant start and a futile end.

Across the broader circle, there were significant differences of opinion about what "good" could look like.

One of the arguments against breaking down silos revolved around accountability. "How is anyone going to be able to work out who is responsible for what?" some questioned.

Then, there were concerns about value attribution: "How are budgets and projects going to be managed if everyone was effectively pulled into a single amalgamated unit?"

Other considerations came from potential implications of over-disclosure – a dilemma reminiscent of my previous debates with Sarah at

BBG. "How are we ever going to be able to ensure that we don't have too much information getting into too many hands?"

However, the most significant concern was focused on the feasibility of the exercise. "This is never going to work," a vocal pro-silo advocate declared with unshakable conviction.

For the inner circle of data practitioners, those early days brought ramifications that went from the professional into the personal. My colleague Stella, for example, had been a senior data engineer but moved into a design and architectural role as part of our early silo restructuring efforts. This was an exciting proposition, in part because it translated to a positional promotion. It also meant a significant increase in her breadth of exposure and more visibility than her previous data engineering position had afforded her. Yet, what was intended to deliver progress – both for the individual and the team – drifted dangerously close to catastrophe.

I suspected that things had begun to unravel when I received an unusual meeting invitation. Soon, I would confirm that Stella had been gripped by a cascade of fears. She had fears about her change of roles, about not being capable of being effective in the new position. Yet, she also had fears that there would be consequences, including impacts on her career progression, if she resisted the move. She feared coming across as a coward to friends and family if she said no, but was also wary about how a potential failure in her new role would impact her personal life.

"I must confess, it got to a point where my mental health started to get significantly impacted," she admitted in our confidential one-to-one meeting. "I didn't know where to turn or whom to trust."

In a work environment where she did not feel safe to disclose even the most mundane of matters, Stella was even less comfortable sharing concerns about her mental well-being. She confided that she had been contending with such fears for years – and that the situation had worsened over time. I felt intense concern when she confessed that she was "heading for a major crisis and desperately needed to do something fast."

During the course of my career, I witnessed many versions of the impact of a company's culture on the well-being of team members, and one aspect kept coming up: resistance to change. In the example of Sarah at BBG, the resistance seemed driven by her fear that the bank's inability to change sufficiently and quickly enough would hinder its ability to deliver on the proposed regulatory demands. These were significant concerns – but they were primarily organisational.

Yet, in Stella's case, I saw that there were very real and very human costs associated with muscling through an agenda related to breaking down silos. Beyond organisational impact, we were seeing a different side: human suffering. I realised that for achieving real and tangible success while limiting negative outfalls for individuals and the organisation at large, something had to change.

The months and years that followed did indeed lead to a significant paradigm shift – and ultimately achieved a radical transformation. There were moments when this seismic technological and cultural transformation was palpable. In one meeting with Fatima, an experienced member of the team who had made her transition from a medium-sized firm to TAG a couple of years before my arrival, I asked for feedback about how our transformation was progressing. She responded that it was beyond any expectations she could reasonably have had. Even more striking was her admission of sometimes "feeling over-empowered." What made this particularly meaningful was that it came from an individual who had previously agonised about a lack of empowerment as well as a misalignment between promises of the hiring committee and her actual role.

There was also the case of Lancelot, the data engineer with expertise in the niche platform. His capabilities and skills, which were extremely scarce and sought-after, had been predominantly amassed at TAG, yet they had not been purposefully shared across the firm. Within months of a targeted intervention, the situation had radically changed. Beyond mitigating the negative consequences of this critical knowledge silo and resource bottleneck, the transformation led to mutually beneficial outcomes and new capability development opportunities were also created.

In addition to reducing much of the previous operation risk, the new order delivered heightened scalability and flexibility. We were able to resolve the issue of the data architects who had developed knowledge silos capable of holding entire business processes to ransom. Within months, data architecture had transformed from a potentially precarious situation to a cooperative environment that felt increasingly stable and secure.

For example, this allowed us to settle the situation with Uduje, who had amassed power by owning a critical reporting system and who had leveraged his position to secure a lucrative financial package. Our organisational transformation – and work on reducing the impact of silos – created enough confidence to eventually allow Uduje to execute on his threat of leaving.

Outcomes also improved for Stella, the senior data engineer who had been compelled to accept a move into a design and architecture role. Shortly after our conversation where she admitted to being close to a major crisis, a focused intervention delivered a beneficial resolution to this delicate situation. I later received a note about her perception of the transformation and her new state of mind. She suggested that while firms recognised the importance of the mental well-being of their employees to their success, it was often not sufficiently prioritised – with lip-service, instead, being paid to the idea. However, she acknowledged that things had changed. She felt the conditions were now right for achieving "a win/win situation for all parties."

Perhaps the most revealing example involved a new team member called Sam, who had only joined us a few months ago. Despite her relatively limited exposure to our technology landscape, we had no hesitation in asking her to help set up some new infrastructure in our recently established cloud environment. In less than six hours, she was done. On the surface, there wasn't anything overly remarkable about this. Yet, in the context of where we'd been only a couple of years before, this would likely have taken six months of planning, six months of trying to secure the budget and another six months to implement the required infrastructure and security changes.

"This just brings to life how very different things have now become," one of my colleagues declared. Even more noteworthy was that Sam, our new team member, had so quickly gained many new skills and was fully embedded across our internationally dispersed teams. It was also impressive that we were now able to deliver modern data services and deploy machine learning and artificial intelligence models into the cloud and at scale.

Only months before, in my heated conversations with Albert, he had compared getting his data science team access to basic information with climbing a mountain. At that time, Sam's speedy success would have been considered an absurd pipedream.

"Why are we even talking about the cloud now when we can't even get the bare essentials to work?" Albert had asked. "Data science in the cloud? Here at TAG? I think it is clear that this will be absolutely unachievable within our lifetimes."

Yet here we were, with both people and technology beginning to interact with significantly less friction. Considerable volumes of data and artificial intelligence capabilities were being developed in parallel. Our pace of change and speed of operational execution had substantially increased. And a framework for enhancing value alignment had been established.

Now, it already seemed difficult to recall the challenges of those early days, when blame was the culture and disempowerment the norm, when change was resisted and health implication increased the pressure, when Jo's service failure with its catastrophic customer implications kick-started a transformation effort that would lead to a seismic paradigm shift, and when that early morning call did much more than jolting me awake.

While those dark days were thankfully behind us now, there remained one conspicuous difference between the originally intended approach and the one that had begun to deliver such successes: our silos had remained unbroken.

6

The Awakening

It was conference season, the period between early spring and midsummer when event organisers look to match the most relevant speakers with the most appropriate venues. I enjoy speaking engagements and connecting with other leaders and, despite turning down a good number of opportunities, I often end up with a challenging schedule.

Yet, a notable example of the rewards of such gatherings comes from one particularly memorable conference in the summer of 2019, where I was able to connect some of the missing pieces. It started like a lot of conferences did in those pre-pandemic times, with lots of material on offer but only a handful of new insights filtering through. This, however, changed when the first set of round tables kicked in just before lunch.

I had chosen a discussion on gender diversity, partly because most of the other options flogged buzz titles that were widely replicated across events, and partly because I was curious about the extreme lack of diversity on display. Before I joined in, there was a solitary male represented among 11 women.

I heard some remarkable stories. The woman sitting to my left kicked off proceedings by sharing her personal experience of being overlooked for over a decade. Her extreme bitterness and pain were impossible to miss as she recounted situations where she had felt invisible – as if nothing she said counted or mattered. Her presentation turned even darker when she disclosed a suicide in her team. After joining the team and promising positive change, a former boss had suddenly taken his own life, leaving his family and the entire team in disarray. Fortunately, a subsequent organisational restructuring delivered outcomes she had no longer imagined possible. Over the last year, a new boss had transformed the work environment in such a way that the woman was now being acknowledged and listened to – she even had her first promotion approved.

DOI: 10.1201/9781003278276-8

There were many touching stories, but another one stood out for presenting evidence on a tangible and broad transformation. It came from the only other man in the group, a senior executive at one of the U.K.'s largest media and telecommunications giants. He shared details about his role in transforming a situation from what some had described as sinister to one that was increasingly safe and harmonious. He talked about implementing radical changes and a raft of new policies.

"When I first arrived from another extremely large firm, it was clear that people meant well. Yet, it was easy to see that things just weren't right," he said. "There were already attempts to balance out senior positions to gain more representation, but most decisions were still being made by the usual suspects."

The senior telecom executive explained that "the usual suspects" were the privileged white male elite that had historically called the shots. However, only a couple of years into a well-sponsored initiative promoting a new set of purposefully crafted codes of conduct, he had seen a marked difference across the organisation.

Prior to the changes, identifying as part of the LGBTQ+ community had put him in what felt like "no one's land," he confessed. Yet while the transformation had sometimes felt forced, it had resulted in a certain sense of mutual respect for all.

About midway through the session, I was put on the spot – I was asked about my team's composition. The answer? Only 20 per cent female representation across my department of over a 100. Some teams didn't even have a single female colleague. On the face of it, my teams were embarrassingly unbalanced.

While I could present a number of reasons for this, any explanation would have been perceived as defensive and potentially unhelpful. I instead disclosed that my senior leadership team was much closer to a 50/50 gender representation.

"That's interesting," one of the roundtable's participants remarked.

> How did that happen? I am particularly intrigued since the stereotypical situation is usually the other way around: a higher female percentage in the general population, with smaller numbers filtering into senior roles. You seem to be describing the opposite situation.

I was indeed describing circumstances that were very different from the norm, but this did not stop the question from catching me out, perhaps because I did not have the kind of story we just heard from the senior telecom executive. I explained our transformation from a culture of blame and finger-pointing to a respectful one where people felt safe. Yet the change had happened organically so I had no theoretical framework to share. Moving from an environment with significant barriers to information flow to one where negative implications of silos were significantly reduced had not come as a result of a highly structured initiative nor a consultancy-firm-led intervention.

However, to paint a picture of the kinds of strange situations I had encountered during my career, I went beyond my recent engagement at TAG to describe an experience associated with a large recruitment drive I had been leading.

The scene unfolded at the Media King, a company with over 12 billion dollars in revenue and more than 30,000 employees, during a period of high growth pressures. An economic windfall – that went against the trend set by the global recession – meant significant increases in demand for my team's services. At the same time, we had been running a number of technology projects to enhance our capability, which meant additional strain on the team as we needed to develop new skills and ways of operating while keeping outputs as close to normal as possible.

On one specific day, I had two interviews in my calendar, with both candidates promising similar backgrounds and experiences. As I got to my feet to head into the back-to-back interviews, I was stopped by a colleague, eager to provide his input on whom he considered the ideal candidate.

"Ed, I trust that you will pick the right one," called out Ahmed Davis, who already had a reputation for being quite radical in his views. Perhaps spotting my perplexed expression, he went on to elaborate, "You know, the one more like us?"

While he was clearly doing his utmost to be clear, his elaboration only served to increase my confusion. I stood stunned for a moment. *Ahmed is a white middle-aged British man who recently married a Muslim woman of Asian origin, subsequently converted to Islam and adopted a religious name befitting to his new identity,* I reflected. *I am a dark-skinned, British Nigerian who rarely discusses ethnicity and seldom debates religious beliefs.*

Ahmed's reference to "like us" didn't immediately yield any insights on the direction of his hiring recommendation.

My face must have shown confusion, so Ahmed approached and whispered, "I meant not the Paki," in close range. Although by no means an isolated occurrence, this incident served as a stark reminder of how openly biased some people still were.

The challenges with the proposed constitution of my senior leadership team at TAG were by no means identical to the Media King situation, yet there also lurked the dangers of bias and discrimination, only this time focused on gender.

While the idea of diverse teams received enthusiastic support from some, there was surprisingly strong resistance from others. At first, this was not obvious. It initially seemed that eligible female candidates across the department were not interested in the positions created by organisational restructuring.

"Why are they so unwilling to put their names forward?" I wondered. "Is this just an extension of our broader organisational culture challenges? Or is there more to this situation than meets the eye?"

I was reminded of some of the patterns I had previously noticed, where *concealed concerns* were hampering progress and presented an opportunity for engagement and intervention. My suspicion was soon confirmed when a regular phone call ended in an emotional meltdown. At the other end of the line was Eki, who had been earmarked to join my leadership team. Unprompted, she shared some very personal insights about her career development. Having been with the firm for many years, Eki had worked with numerous line managers over the years.

"I don't know if I can do this, Ed," she said.

> In my heart, I want this, and feel that I might be able to do it. But I have just been put down so much and have been so repeatedly overlooked that I just seem to have developed some underlying fears that I am doomed to fail, if I was being honest.

She described how, regardless of her efforts and personal sense of achievements, she had never been acknowledged or recognised by any of her managers in a pattern that repeated again and again.

Eki said,

> One manager kept promising that things would change but in all honesty, they just never did. Not one of his promises ever got fulfilled, and then it got even worse. He started to avoid me. Monthly one-to-one meetings got pushed further and further away, and then they got cancelled altogether.

As Eki dug into these painful memories, the sadness in her voice became increasingly obvious. But when her recollections shifted to the conclusions she had reached, sadness turned to anger. Eki told me that, again and again, her peers got the promotions she had been promised, that others took the credit for work that she had put in, that her ideas were sometimes claimed by her bosses without any acknowledgement of her contribution. At the same time, she felt she was often set up for failure and given tasks that had no chance of delivering positive results. When she looked at the patterns of team members getting promoted over her, it was obvious that there was some gender bias at play.

"The one thing I would say is that of the many who seemed to be favoured over me, not one was female," she said.

Was this just a coincidence? I wondered. How has this cycle of perpetual disregard been overlooked for so long? How could this level of gender discrimination have gone unnoticed? I also wondered why Eki had, by her own admission, never opened up about any of this.

"If I was being absolutely honest with myself, I think I was just afraid," she said. Among her many fears were concerns about potential implications for her career trajectory – about how speaking out may have affected her prospects for promotions or year-end bonuses. In hindsight, she felt that none of this actually mattered. She received no recognition, and the career progression never materialised.

Based on this string of seemingly endless disappointments, it was easy to see why she felt her efforts were always destined to lead to futility.

It must have been incredibly difficult to contend with such thoughts, fears and concerns for so long, I imagined, especially as they seemed destined to remain concealed. I also recalled another meeting with Mikael, a senior finance executive. His strong reservations, which he raised in strict confidence, gave me a clear indication that an internal resistance to diverse teams was very real.

The meeting started in the usual way, with a review of high-priority projects. It was a period of heightened anxiety as a regulatory deadline was fast approaching. But since we were on track – and progress remained predictable – there seemed to be a reasonable level of confidence, which made his worried demeanour all the more puzzling. Soon it became evident that his concerns had nothing to do with the delivery of these critical projects but were centred on proposals for the restructuring of the data department.

"Can we speak off the record," he suddenly asked. This was an intriguing turn of events since our sessions were held in confidence by default. We also enjoyed a reasonably close working relationship, yet here he was, struggling to formulate his point.

It soon became clear that he had concerns about potential impacts on my team's interaction with the finance department and was keen to be reassured that the proposed changes would not create new frictions. As I listened closely to the issues he raised and worked through each item with him, the level of anxiety in the room was progressively dissipated. One concern, however, was not so easily addressed. We found ourselves stuck with divergent views about one of the candidates for a key operational role: Eki.

Mikael had significant reservations about her ability to fulfil this role. He was particularly concerned since this area of responsibility included frequent interaction with finance teams.

I was keen to explore these concerns, especially since they were raised by an important stakeholder whom I considered a potential key ally, yet it was difficult to deduce what was at the root of his discomfort. He only seemed able to express unsubstantiated anecdotal allegations. In effect, he just had an uncomfortable gut feeling. Why was he so concerned? Perhaps more importantly, why was it so challenging to bring any underlying issues into the open?

"This might be difficult to explain, Ed," he suggested. "But let's give it a try."

Not only was it difficult to get to the reasons behind Mikael's reservations, his position also seemed at odds with the bulk of the internal references I had received about Eki. Multiple sources provided predominantly positive comments about her work, describing her as "a gem, hardworking, undervalued, dedicated, loyal to the end, and always putting customers first."

Now I wondered whether there were others who felt like Mikael, who were deeply uncomfortable with the rapid transformation that was underway. Were there others struggling to articulate their deeply *concealed concerns*?

This exploration was eye-opening since it gave me a clear indication that support for diversifying teams could not be taken for granted or assumed by default. It also brought back memories of the encounter with Ahmed at the Media King, who attempted to influence a recruitment drive towards people "more like us." I remember how difficult it was to fully comprehend his underlying concerns about other candidates.

I also recalled other encounters that suggested a pattern where situations which could be perceived as discriminatory were closely linked to *concealed concerns*.

After lunch, it was my turn to moderate a round-table discussion with the central question, "What makes for an ideal data foundation for Artificial Intelligence?"

The conversation inspired some exciting and unorthodox revelations. It started with the usual denunciation of silos, which were often blamed when things went wrong, within organisations as well as at conferences.

"The biggest problem within my organisation are the silos between various departments," a healthcare executive declared. "It is literally costing us hundreds of millions of dollars worldwide. It significantly slows down the flow of information across the firm and most certainly limits progress with artificial intelligence and data science initiatives."

She indicated that her organisation was at the point where many initiatives to break down silos had shown very low levels of tangible results. The reason, she believed, came from people who, on the surface, wanted change yet were unwilling to implement any changes that might individually affect them.

"I feel your pain," said another participant, who introduced herself as the chief operating officer of a well-known cancer charity. She shared experiences of how silos within her company had meant that no figures or reports could be taken at face value.

"We now have armies of people who spend disproportionate amounts of their bandwidth validating and verifying numbers," she said, lamenting the resources wasted on identifying and fixing data issues that could have otherwise been dedicated to advancing core competencies.

"I have analysts who can't analyse, data scientists who struggle to do much data science and visualisation experts who spend most of their time visualising data discrepancies," she said. "All ultimately caused by our challenges with silos."

At that point, another participant jumped in to tell a similar story, reinforcing the impression that the entire group's viewpoint – that silos were bad and had to be dismantled at all costs – was aligned and consistent. After much discussion about silos and resistance to organisational change, there was one suggestion that resonated with me.

It came from Mark, the global chief digital officer of one of the world's most respected luxury brands, who said that he saw microservices as intentional – and well-functioning examples of silos. I found the analogy fascinating.

Microservices are small, autonomous, independent and decentralised technology implementations that are developed with self-contained pieces of business functionality and clearly defined interfaces that enable seamless interactions with the world beyond their external walls. Popularised through the success stories from technology behemoths like Google, Netflix, Facebook and Amazon, this approach to implementing technology is increasingly adopted across industry sectors and all kinds of firms.

The idea, first proposed in 2005 by Peter Rodgers, the originator of resource-oriented computing, had gained more prominence in recent years. With the increasing complexity of legacy technology systems, this didn't come as a surprise. Over the years, technology systems and landscapes have become bulkier and more difficult to manage, update and maintain. The microservices approach is a relatively new way of addressing these challenges by splitting up complex technology applications into autonomous building blocks or modular services. Unlike their monolithic legacy predecessors, these modular services can be independently developed, deployed and managed. They can also be combined to deliver rich functionality. Beyond this, such modern systems are incredibly resilient, accessible, maintainable, adaptable and scalable. They are actually easier to integrate than traditionally large single-unit systems.

It was interesting to reflect on this move, led by the world's biggest innovators, from single-system landscapes towards microservices, essentially from a world of consolidation towards one of decoupled silos.

Mark went on to describe how he was driving a transformation towards silos within his organisation. "Modern systems not only need to be able to contend with silos, they in fact need to actively and intentionally create them," he said.

It struck me that the approach to transforming modern systems, as he outlined it, was not limited to technology. It also applied to people and to processes.

He went as far as suggesting that such modern systems were the only way for forward-thinking organisations to realise their ambitions.

"Look, I can categorically say that given all the experience I've had across technology, and given the catastrophic failures I've seen across numerous companies, silos are the only way to achieve true high-speed and low-friction scale." Mark paused for a few seconds, before adding, "But there has to be an intentional and well-conceived approach to either creating new silos or adapting old ones."

He was, in effect, advocating for the unbreaking of silos – a 360-degree departure from commonly held views across executives, firms and sectors.

For many years, I had contemplated it, researched it and even experimented with it, but this was the first time that I witnessed open and public support for this radically different approach.

Indeed, rather than joining the ubiquitary call to break down silos, I had often spoken up about their benefits, especially in regard to enabling the kinds of adaptability and scale that firms were hoping to achieve. Although his declaration echoed my own thoughts, it felt particularly bold nonetheless. I had no doubt Mark's reasoning made sense and the underpinning principles were sound, yet I wondered if the others could also be persuaded.

He then shared anecdotes about how intentionally limiting the size of agile teams had helped to increase flexibility and adaptability while maintaining autonomy. As a well-respected digital executive, Mark also positioned the technological equivalents of both service-oriented architecture and microservice architecture as somewhat analogous to the premise of creating silos.

"It's really interesting to hear this," I interjected. "For years now, I also have considered silos as great tools, because they can be incredibly focused, specialised and internally adaptable. However, they can also be the absolute antithesis of deft when they are not effectively and seamlessly connected."

Mark nodded in agreement, but a look around the table showed that a number of participants were quite uncomfortable with what they were hearing.

As rare as our positions on silos seemed to be, I soon learned that we were not the only conference participants sharing such views. Over a coffee break later that day, an experienced data specialist and sought-after independent consultant, who introduced himself as George, confessed to having eavesdropped on our conversation.

"I was sitting at a table adjacent to yours and I caught aspects of some of the thoughts you shared," said George, confessing that he had been tempted to switch tables at a point but had abandoned the idea since it might have been considered rude or downright disruptive.

"In a world of herd mindsets, it was highly commendable of you to reiterate the overlooked opportunities that silos and federated repositories are capable of delivering," he said.

George described how he had applied similar concepts to deliver successful outcomes for his clients. "I would say it is now pretty much impossible to craft or design robust technology architectures, based solely on advancements in innovations such as publisher versus subscriber frameworks," he said, arguing that benefits would instead be dependent on well-defined taxonomies, governance and matured ways of thinking about systems design.

When the round-table discussion resumed, the head of data for a healthcare company suggested that she also saw lots of benefits from keeping silos across her organisation intact.

"I have to admit that I have never considered silos this broadly and have never been able to propose the more general positive implications of silos as you have just suggested," she said. "However, my team and I find the kind of tight controls that data segregation provides very beneficial from a data protection and data privacy standpoint."

She described how she had been resistant towards the notion of breaking down silos – and how the status quo had made complying with increasing data regulation much more achievable.

Unexpectedly, the idea of intentional silos was gathering more and more support among the group. "This is music to my ears," said the chief information and cyber security officer for a big retailer.

> It often feels like I am a lone fighter in the battle to keep our silos in place. Pretty much everyone else in my organisation seems to think silos are something out of the stone ages, some even go as far as considering them evil.

This was fascinating. Not only were silos receiving vocal support, but they came from two different perspectives. On the one hand, there were those who considered silos essential for the effective control and protection of a firm's information assets. These were the more traditional positions – defensive of the status quo – as illustrated by the comments from the chief information and cyber security officer and the healthcare head of data.

Others, on the other hand, were more focused on forward-looking benefits. For example, there was the idea that modern systems not only needed to contend with silos but actively and intentionally create them, according to Mark, who had also implied that such modern systems were not limited to technology but also applied to people and processes. He also noted that he saw intentional silos as the only way for organisations to realise their ambitions of achieving high speed and low friction.

For the first time, I was in the company of credible experts from a variety of sectors who were all in agreement that silos could make beneficial contributions to their firms. However, their perspectives were vastly different, ranging from concerns about protecting the status quo to succeeding in an increasingly fast-paced and competitive environment.

The viewpoints mirrored some of my professional experiences across multiple organisations. At TAG, the risk and compliance teams were keen to preserve silos as they considered silos essential tools for protecting "the crown jewels" of the organisation. While regulatory frameworks, such as the European Union General Data Protection Regulation, focus on ensuring robust controls for personal and sensitive information, "crown jewels" cover a much broader scope – they include any data or information assets that could adversely impact a firm's competitive advantage or inflict damage to the organisation's reputation.

Risk and compliance teams were extremely sceptical about the idea of breaking down silos. They feared that a more open landscape would increase the organisation's vulnerability – and potentially lead to damage to the firm's brand and increased risks to its bottom line.

Another situation came to mind from the time when I was engaged with a global property services firm. It was one of the world's largest commercial real estate service organisations, which was close to the top end of the Fortune 500 index back then and had over 90,000 employees delivering services to clients in more than 80 countries.

However, due to its broad range of services, it often found itself representing the interests of competing clients, which required the purposeful erection of so-called Chinese walls to mitigate the risk of damaging leaks. Such intentional silos of different teams working with different brands or client portfolios were vitally important for non-disclosure purposes and to avoid potential conflicts of interest.

Yet compliance teams were not the only source of resistance to breaking down silos at the firm. Speaking with local sales teams, I discovered that the implication of data sharing was a real concern for the exclusive ownership of customers and the appropriation of fee commissions. As commission and fee structures were jurisdictionally and individually aligned, internal sales teams and individual salespeople were in the uncomfortable position of being in competition with one another.

"It sometimes feels much easier to share information with my network across industry than to exchange data among colleagues within my own firm," a sales manager based in the Paris office once told me.

The mandate – coming from the senior executive team – was to break down silos completely in order to realise growth in new revenues, estimated to amount to millions of dollars, from boundless data sharing.

Proponents of this vision campaigned for the complete demolition of interdepartmental boundaries and promoted a "one company" approach. I recall one team member expressing his disgust at finding it easier to get information related to some of our deals inventory from external – rather than internal – sources.

"Would you believe that I often get wind of deals that we might be getting involved in, and leads that could be good targets, from external sources even before any internal information is forthcoming?" he complained.

Others, however, remained opposed to dismantling silos and were desperate to uphold the status quo.

And then there were those who sat on the fence. They were open to compromise and happy to consider proposals, where data fields could be classified based on sensitivity ratings agreed upon with data owners who were typically country or business line managers. In one such proposal, data assets would be tagged either "red, amber or green." The green tag indicated data that could be shared across business lines and geographical boundaries without compromising compliance, confidentiality or other data accessibility considerations. In other words, this was data that the firm was happy to place in the public domain.

The amber designation meant that data could only be shared within predefined internal or external communities – across business lines and/ or geographical boundaries. A robust data accessibility model would articulate any groups that should have access to such data.

Data classified as red could not be shared externally – and in most cases even internally – under ordinary circumstances, with any release of such data requiring explicit authorisation through a rigorous data governance framework.

In this proposal, data owners had the flexibility to define and categorise the data within their scope of accountability.

I had witnessed many variations of firms' efforts to address the silo conundrum. Perhaps the most radical approach was the "open by default" paradigm I encountered in my role as a consultant for a public-sector client. This revolutionary idea was an attempt to shake up the common inertia associated with data-sharing initiatives. The standard convention was that data was "closed by default," putting the onus on the persons requesting data to "justify to disclose" any data sets that they might require access to.

The new approach proposed the other extreme, where data was "open by default" with the onus shifted to the data owner to "justify to conceal" any data assets they had reason to withhold.

This felt remarkably close to the idea of a "boundaryless organisation," as envisioned by Jack Welch, the then-CEO of GE more than 25 years ago.

"Our dream for the 1990s is a boundaryless company," he wrote in GE's 1990 annual report to shareholders. "A company where we knock down the walls that separate us from each other on the inside and from our key constituencies on the outside."

His ambition was to inspire creative collaboration across his entire workforce with the hope that this might bring together people from different levels, departments and locations. He was driven by the conviction that "silo free" organisations were essential to enable the appropriation of the benefits of emergent globalisation and technological innovation.

Yet, despite the initial euphoria surrounding Welch's concept, boundaries have remained intact in the vast majority of firms. Most organisations still find that divisions and silos remain deeply entrenched in hierarchical processes and that practices are fragmented.

The ubiquitous silo mentality, which has plagued organisations and impacted their ability to rapidly adapt to changing conditions, correlates with a reluctance to share information with different departments and across various teams. For most companies, progress towards reaching the holy grail of a seamlessly collaborative organisation as envisioned by Welch has been calcified by rhetoric and has failed to make a fulsome transition to a tangible reality.

I found it fascinating to reflect on the different, even contradictory, approaches of Jack Welch and Peter Rodgers, who both seemed focused on the same outcome: the elimination of interactional frictions. In some ways, Rodgers' idea of microservices could be seen as the opposite of Welch's "boundaryless organisation."

After all, Rogers suggested erecting intentional boundaries when Welch proposed knocking them down. One sought a deliberate decomposition into functional components of a large system and the other focused on recomposition – effectively pitting systemic consolidation against the idea of systemic separation, of "breaking big things into small things."

Analogous to the idea of microservices – and particularly the approach of "breaking big things into small things" – are the increasingly popular practices of agile in software development.

Agile, an iterative approach to project management, was first put forward by a group of 17 renowned software developers who met at a Utah resort in 2001. Their proposal was a response to the prevailing methods of the time, which were perceived to be excessively regulated, over-planned and micro-managed. Such heavyweight methods, collectively referred to as "waterfall," were typically saddled with significant upfront overheads and a substantial administrative burden, culminating in a "throw it over the wall" approach.

In contrast, proponents of agile called for "breaking big things into small things," light-touch administration, just sufficient documentation and collaborative cross-functional teams. Contrary to some perceptions, agile is not defined by a set of ceremonies or specific development techniques. Instead, it is derived from a group of methodologies, such as Scrum and Kanban, some of which can be traced back to the mid-1950s, that demonstrate a commitment to tight feedback cycles and continuous improvement.

What some may not be aware of is that the fundamental ideology and principles foundational to agile software development have become widely applied in general management. They have progressively filtered into areas like strategy, governance, risk and finance, where they can be recognised by terms such as business agility and agile business management. Beyond business applications, Bruce Feiler's TED Talk highlighted how the principles underpinning agile paradigms have been used in other areas of life, like raising children, for example. Such broader uses draw on some of the fundamental tenets of agile management: trust, communication, collaboration, adaptation, awareness and "breaking big things into small things" among them.

A common thread across the methodologies and practices based on agile principles is their advocacy for "breaking big things into small things" in order to increase efficiency for realising tangible outcomes. Beyond implementing an intentional systemic separation to interactions with stakeholders, the gathering of requirements, the planning of work, the execution of plans, and the lifecycle of delivery, these practices are also very stringent on conditions about team size. They mandate the breaking up of big teams or the formation of small teams, deliberately creating autonomous entities with clearly defined borders – which arguably contradicts the idea of a "boundaryless organisation."

Both models of organisational mindsets seem focused on the same outcome – the elimination of interactional frictions – but take opposite approaches to resolution. While one model is focused on a mission to dismantle and eradicate silos, the other promotes their creation and preservation.

By the end of our 45-minute round-table discussion, a convergence of perspectives became evident, yet one big question stayed in the room, "How to achieve a successful organisational transformation in practice?"

Early in the debate, the views around the table seemed insurmountably divided. Yet, as time progressed, shared experiences and common challenges served to draw participants closer – as if by an unseen magnetic pull – to a point much closer to alignment. Yet, as proceedings came to a close, I could not help but wonder what this consensus was pointing towards. Were we a judging panel for the purpose of declaring a winner or loser among two competing approaches? And if so, were we truly judging the contestants by keeping the most essential guiding question – "to what end" – in mind?

My mind flashed back to the heated conversations with Albert at TAG, which had initially revolved around the breaking down of silos. However, when our focus shifted away from a fixation on silos and towards what we were actually looking to achieve, we were able to accelerate our drive towards tangible progress. This was no isolated incident. I have seen this pattern repeated in countless situations and across numerous organisational settings. In each of these cases, making the transition away from fears or concerns and towards purpose or "to what end" invariably led to a path towards resolution.

Part III

A Path Towards Resolution

Exploring Experiential Solutions for Achieving Effective Mindset Shifts

7

The Wars of the Roses

For over a quarter of a century, silos have been associated with so much hampered growth and escalated costs across firms and organisations that they're widely considered a plague. The symptoms are numerous – and include increased organisational rigidity, lower productivity, a diminished ability to adapt to changing market conditions, dwindling morale and growing difficulties to realise the full benefits of technological advancements, such as artificial intelligence, the internet of things and blockchain.

Yet, rather than joining the pervading calls to "break down silos," I am proposing a different – and potentially controversial – approach. By shifting the attention from the plague to the perceived symptoms, I believe that firms are able to craft tangible and viable solutions.

However, the insights presented in this book don't come from a place of grandeur or arrogance. Instead, they are born from deep-seated humility and draw on my diverse background and experience coupled with the creative perspective this combination has facilitated over the years.

The examples illustrate my experience that so far, every attempt of breaking down silos has led to futility – and sometimes went even further. In some cases, the intention to rattle the status quo brought not only negative psychological consequences but triggered even more resistance. This caused silos to become more deeply rooted and more isolated, with their surrounding walls becoming even more impenetrable.

Instead of adopting a mission to disintegrate or disaggregate functional structures, including silos, I believe better outcomes can be gained from intentionally protecting the internal integrity of independent structures that demonstrate individual functional robustness.

At the same time, it is clear that the broadest achievable benefits for an organisation – and for the individuals who enable organisational existence – would be out of reach without reducing or even eliminating

DOI: 10.1201/9781003278276-10

the friction from the interactions between individuals and groups, and between items and collectives.

Of my numerous encounters with the silo conundrum, one incident stands out. Not long after I had joined TAG as head of data, I found myself in a lose-lose situation with a disgruntled senior data scientist. He was extremely frustrated about the many hurdles he and his team had to cross in order to get things done. He questioned why the simple seemed so complicated, why the efforts of his team had been so severely hampered by the prevalence of silos across our organisation.

Another telling moment happened when a meeting between financial regulators and bankers suddenly escalated to become an intense battle. Held at the offices of BBG, the encounter took place not long after the catastrophic crash of Lehman Brothers that inflicted unprecedented damage on the world's entire financial system. On the surface, the meeting's impassioned debates revolved around the topic of whether some banks and financial institutions were "too big to fail," ignited by a fear that increasing regulatory disclosure demands might impede the ability of financial firms to deliver services for their customers. I would later discover that there was more to the crossfire than what it seemed on the surface.

While every encounter was unique, a common thread appeared to stitch all of them together. In hindsight, I discovered that by shifting attention away from a fixation on silos and towards the greater purpose, we made more – and faster – headway towards resolution.

In the case of BBG, this meant turning our attention to concerns about the organisation's challenging technology landscape and prevalent interactional frictions, which choked the channels of exchange between one part of the firm and another. What looked like a debate about disclosure revealed concerns about significant underlying cultural issues, which had been deeply concealed at the time.

TAG's goals were twofold. One, to enhance operational resilience by not only reducing the risks of failure but also ensuring a faster response should failures occur. Two, to increase its ability to adapt to changing market conditions and to maximise the impact of new technologies for turning new ideas into products or services. These goals underpinned the firm's ambition to drive effective growth and profitability.

Rather than supporting any argument on either side of the discussions about silos, I have found it more useful to look beyond the silo conundrum – towards the intended outcomes. A focus on a firm's ambitions, purpose, goals and clear propositions of "to what end" is more useful for devising solutions and creating value, I believe.

Yet, how do we define the purpose of a firm? For a fuller understanding, I decided to look into history. The archives of the British-born economist Ronald Coase seemed a good place to start. His influential 1937 essay on *The Nature of the Firm*, which earned him a Nobel Prize, explored why firms existed. From the premises that "production could be carried on without any organization at all" and that "the price mechanism should give the most efficient result," he concluded that firms exist for the purpose of reducing transaction costs, such as the cost of sourcing and acquiring information, the cost of protecting intellectual property and trade secrets, the cost of negotiating and bargaining for the acquisition of various requirements for production or the cost of managing resources and of legal enforcements. The idea was simple: if more factors of production could be brought under the ownership or control of a single entrepreneurial entity, it would cost less to deliver goods or services to the market. The internalisation of transaction costs by vertically integrating specialised silos of building blocks and resources ultimately lead to increased economies of scale, creating cost advantages for firms through expanding or scaling their operations. It can be useful to consider that each specialised productive input – such as a raw material, a specific element of technology, an individual skill or a data set – can be considered a silo. With this assumption, Coase's findings would suggest that firms exist for the purpose of gaining economic advantages by owning, managing and integrating silos.

If economies of scale – achieved by vertically integrating more and more inputs for production – led to a decrease in the cost per unit of output, why would firms not indefinitely continue to increase in size to achieve global market dominance?

The answer is simple: friction. As more and more vertical inputs are integrated – and the extent of control over such inputs is consolidated – firms initially experience a marginal increase in cost advantages on each unit of their productive output. Yet, as a firm gets larger, the frictions incurred from the interactions between its individual parts accumulate. Left unresolved, these interactional frictions can become increasingly costly to manage. Initially, they may lead to marginal reductions in the overall returns on an organisation's investments. Yet, progressively diminishing returns can push a firm to a tipping point where any additional increase in scale could lead to negative returns.

Over the years, I've witnessed the impact of interactional frictions on numerous organisations, including the global bank BBG and the universal insurer TAG. These experiences suggest that the negative implications of organisational silos could, if left unchecked, be far more damaging than the frustrations I witnessed among stakeholders like Albert and Sarah. Beyond limiting a firm's ability to scale and to grow, such negative outfalls could cause a significant reduction in a firm's competitive advantage – and could ultimately lead to its demise.

It is also important to note that – while firms historically assumed that the transaction costs that needed to be reduced were primarily physical – interactional costs in today's world are increasingly multifaceted. For instance, there are costs associated with not knowing how to best customise an organisation's offering to the specific demands of its target customers. Not being able to get the right products to market – at the right time and the right price point – also comes with costs. There are also significant costs to not being flexible enough to adapt to the changing demands of an organisation's customer base or to the markets within which it operates.

The success of a firm is no longer solely dependent on the amount of capital it can amass or the number of resources it can acquire. Instead, business outcomes are increasingly dependent on the firm's ability to limit the interactional friction that builds up between the individual silos that are part of its operations. In other words, for organisations to stay competitive in an increasingly complex world, they need to reduce the things that hinder the "flow of materials" – as was the historical focus – and also remove impediments to the "flows of information."

Only by reducing frictions across silos can firms operate efficiently – and ultimately find success in today's markets and those of the future.

However, unlike many other organisational challenges, the issue of silos has not been addressed with the same vigour and innovative advancements that have helped to transform the way leading organisations operate. Instead, silos have remained a central issue that executives and management teams across firms of all sizes grapple with, often in isolation from other pertinent organisational challenges.

During my career, I have seen the ills of silos manifested across a variety of industries, including banking, retail, commercial finance, agriculture, insurance, environmental, public finance, entertainment, utilities, media, talent recruitment, hospitality, real estate, consulting and the multilateral sector.

I've come across cases where internal groupings and collectives encapsulated within organisational boundaries are characterised by a poor level of vertical integration with other silos and, in extreme cases, become virtually impenetrable from other parts of the organisation. Such groupings and collectives can include systems, processes, functions, departments and teams – all operating in isolation from others outside their imposed borders.

Over the years, thoughts about silos and their implications for organisations have turned to data, which is now widely considered a foundational denominator for intrinsic value. Data captured within individual silos typically represent considerable value for particular user groups. At the same time, such data is not always accessible for use outside the predefined perimeter. Such restrictions hamper the interactions between silos and other human or technology systems across the organisation, which can have a range of consequences.

In some organisations, silos can lead to employees being unable to gain access to data that is outside of their departments, teams or functional boundaries, potentially to the extent that team members find it more feasible to acquire data from external – rather than internal – sources.

At TAG, one of these internal impediments to the "flow of information" led to a court case against a suspect accused of being a serial insurance fraudster. Within the first few weeks of joining the firm, I kicked off an extensive series of workshops aimed at capturing various perspectives on the role of data for supporting the twin ambitions of driving growth and profitability.

One session – bringing together stakeholders from a number of areas, including marketing, fraud, human resource management, technology and finance – started with a question about the biggest challenges the individuals, and the departments they represented, currently had to contend with. This prompted a flood of painful accounts, such as efforts spent on data validation, business disruptions due to poor data service availability, poor access to data insights that would enable improved market qualification and enhanced targeting – and even broader implications on integrity and trust, most of which were attributed to the persistence of silos. Yet perhaps the most intriguing story was relayed by Clive, a representative from the fraud department.

"I honestly don't know where to start," Clive said, his frustration impossible to miss. "Let me share a story that illustrates how bad things have become."

Clive recounted a painful experience that involved taking a customer to court for fraud. "We had placed this gentleman on our blacklist as one of the most persistently blatant fraudsters we had been tracking for a while," he said, describing how his department had – through a number of external collaborations – finally detected a pattern and collected sufficient evidence to take the man to court.

"We were confident that we had a watertight case, but we expected the defendant to attack some of the evidence we presented," Clive explained. "We were surprised when he didn't do that. Instead, he bided his time until the end, when he was able to take centre stage. That's when he landed a bombshell."

Clive described his utter bewilderment when the fraudster landed his trump card.

"Unbeknownst to us, while we were painstakingly putting together an extensive case to nail this notorious individual, he had received no fewer than three promotional messages, inviting him to renew existing products as well as promoting other opportunities."

Clive continued, "The man told the court, 'If I really were such a bad customer as the evidence presented thus far would suggest, why would this firm be so desperate to sell me new products?'"

It was a sensational case, and it illustrated how interactional frictions among individual silos within the organisation had hampered the flow of information to the point where sales and marketing teams had insufficient access to the data points that could have diminished the risk of such costly, wasteful and otherwise damaging encounters.

While the story of the fraudster was particularly striking, it had strong similarities to many of the other challenges – all revolving around silos – presented at the workshop. Silos had yet again led to organisational disjointedness, hindering the implementation of a strategy where data is linked to generating insights, enhancing opportunities and reducing risks.

In recent times, the debate has evolved even further – to the point where silos are now seen as embodiments of the frictions and inertias that hamper organisations. In some instances, the term "silo" is applied, more broadly, to a way of working that is baked into defined circles within a firm and that can be distinctly different from – or incompatible with – other circles within the organisational boundaries.

Our view of organisational silos has broadened and evolved, from an origin in the realms of systems and process – via the data underpinning the codification of definitions and interactions – to the people and cultures that ultimately embody a firm.

Over time, there have been numerous arguments against the existence of silos, with some of their biggest critics pointing at their effects on a firm's ability to adapt to changing demands. Those opposed to silos contend that they limit a firm's flexibility by significantly increasing rigidity and inertia, especially among large and well-established organisations that are more prone to struggling to drive tangible transformations.

At one end of the spectrum, proponents believe that silos can offer some significant benefits to a firm. They can, for example, increase an organisation's ability to exert appropriate controls over valuable information assets. Such arguments point to the need to maintain adequate privacy of customer data, yet there is also evidence that silos can be useful for the protection of an organisation's competitive assets and maintaining a competitive advantage. These viewpoints reflect the sentiments expressed by the senior executives participating in a roundtable.

Arguments in favour of keeping old structures in place, for example, for controlling and protecting a firm's information assets, on the one hand, were typically put forward by executives with accountabilities, such as information security, compliance and cyber protection. The more forward-looking benefits, on the other hand, often found support from people whose mandates spread across areas, such as digital, data, product, sales, marketing and artificial intelligence transformation. These executives would argue that the approach of intentionally preserving silos – or even creating new ones – was the only way for organisations to realise their ambitions of true high-speed and low-friction scale.

Other voices were calling attention to the fact that silos typically enable absolute focus on a specific use or function, which can be particularly useful for adequate scope management and product engineering – and for the iterative delivery of tangible value. Due to their narrow focus and specialisation, silos are particularly efficient for achieving their intended or associated purposes, an attribute that can lead to demonstrable improvements in the quality of delivered outcomes.

There seemed to be no end in sight to the debates for or against silos. Those advocating for integration were embarking on a crusade for the wholesale dismantling of silos while those promoting autonomy were on a mission to not only preserve existing but create new silos. What I found striking, however, was that both sides of this polarising debate were aligned on one central goal: achieving the most appropriate intersection between *interactional speed* and *frictionless scale.*

Both perspectives had valid points, after all, significant benefits can be gained from tight integration as well as strong autonomy. The core challenge? Finding the intersection between *interactional speed* and *frictionless scale,* which requires both *autonomy* and *integration.* Was there a way we could have the best of both worlds? Could we be focused and efficient, yet adaptable and connected? Could we devise a credible approach to resolving this paradox?

From the challenges I witnessed throughout my career, I realised that for countless individuals and leaders across industry sectors, resolving this dilemma was becoming an inflection point for the kind of tangible and transformational change most firms require to stay relevant in today's new economic landscape.

In our efforts to drive towards achieving *interactional speed* and *frictionless scale* at TAG, an additional paradox had to be addressed. We had inherited a group of highly capable individuals, who had amassed a significant body of knowledge over the years. At the same time, individuals with contemporary skills and fresh ideas were also needed. Across firms that are good at retaining talent, like TAG, there are team members who are willing to see change happen in principle, yet they have never seen things done differently. This may leave them with limited reference points for contextualising transformation and for formulating a path forward. In these cases, sharing stories and experiences can be a vital tool for illustrating not only a vision of transformation but also potential strategies for achieving it.

There is no shortage of stories of über-successful firms like Facebook, Amazon, Apple, Netflix and Google, otherwise known by the acronym FAANG, as coined by CNBC Mad Money's Jim Cramer in reference to their unparalleled prominence and market dominance. Yet, such stories often come across as fantastical rather than tangible and humanly achievable. Instead, I have found it more constructive to share relevant personal stories and anecdotes from a broad range of encounters. Tangential analogies can also be useful for advancing understanding, especially when desirable outcomes are shown alongside contrasting examples.

One such analogy highlights a juxtaposition in a mobile phone network. For illustrating the foundational flexibility of such a network, it considers the difference between filling a grid of pipes with concrete versus filling them in with water. Mobile phone networks have the characteristics of being both flexible and solid at the same time. Simply put, it only requires the establishment of additional cell sites to enable service expansion into ever-broader coverage areas.

Likewise, for finding the desirable intersection between *autonomy* and *integration*, it pays to contemplate the establishment of a framework that is different from those that have become the traditional legacies of most firms. Such frameworks would ensure that business teams – and the systems they rely on – are not hemmed in by obstacles that impede the realisation of the combined goals of *interactional speed* and *frictionless scale*. These frameworks would also help to address blockages to the flow of information across silos, which hamper the expedient delivery of organisational outcomes. Today's technology landscape makes this much easier, especially due to the Cloud with its enabling big data and artificial intelligence service capabilities.

Back to the example of a cellular phone network, which seamlessly allows new devices to be brought online and others taken offline – with no noticeable disruption to the rest of the network. Every mobile phone is discretely separate, effectively able to act as a silo in our hands, yet unmistakably interconnected to the entire network when it's required to interact with other devices.

Similar to a mobile phone network, successfully achieving the combined goals of *interactional speed* and *frictionless scale* across a firm's landscape would mean that products and services can be added or removed without adverse impacts on the rest of the operation. In such a framework, each product or service would exist as its own unit or entity – and maintain a level of desirable autonomy – while being integrated into the firm's operational system at the same time.

Another fitting analogy comes from research into the inner workings of our brains. Contemporary science suggests that our brains are the single largest data storage systems in the world. A Stanford University study found that our neurons, the brain cells primarily responsible for storage, processing and transportation of information, have sufficient capacity to store our movie needs for the next couple of years. However, it is the synapses – the bridges that facilitate the connections between these neurons – that enable a 25-fold increase in this capacity.

Due to this exponential increase in capacity, our brains can store information equivalent to over 300 years of continuous Netflix video streaming. Perhaps equally fascinating is the fact that every one of these 80 billion neuronic nerve cells individually has the ability to operate in any one of three states: *broadcast, whisper* or *silence*. The scientific discovery nicknamed "cracking the neural code" found that the brain's nerve cells use the *silence*, acquired in their quiet time, for important activities such as encoding a train of thought, formulating a set of actions or encrypting information. The *whispers* operate differently. They facilitate precise one-to-one exchanges delivering "secret" information, which are transmitted directly from one neuron to another and which travel at a speed far greater than the world's fastest land mammal via a synaptic bridge that acts as the interface. Brain scientists consider these intimate interactions to be homologous to "wired transmission" that enable a light switch to interact with a light bulb.

In comparison, the brain's *broadcast* operations are quite similar to the interactions between an individual mobile phone and its network. These neural operations are thought to influence such basal activities as our energy levels or our perceived ability to carry out a specific activity. In contrast to the most meticulously targeted chemical exchange between a specific nerve cell and another – enabling a *whisper* – a neuron initiates a *broadcast* by the indiscriminate release of chemicals into the fluids that fill the spaces between brain cells. Much like the workings of Wi-Fi or home broadband service, this initiates an unbounded diffusion across our entire brain, dispersing the intended message as if it were a "public announcement."

These insights show that our brains naturally achieve the kind of win-win situation firms can benefit from: with units acting as *autonomous* silos when appropriate and seamlessly switching to being *integrated* when required. What this analogy shows us is that interactional flows across organisational barriers can benefit from enabling and enhancing synaptic connectivity.

Beyond these analogies, I find it useful – and even reassuring – to have personally experienced how mindset shifts yield incredible outcomes.

One of the most remarkable transformations from "disastrous to desirable" I have seen came after the unwelcome wake-up call in my days as head of data at TAG. The immediate aftermath of the incident was marked by mayhem: dreadful impacts on the customer experience and potentially far-reaching implications for reputational risks caused a grim and panicked atmosphere across the firm. Yet what followed was a turnaround that was quicker than what our most ambitious optimists anticipated. We soon had not only addressed our critical emergency but had begun to see tangible outcomes from a cultural reinvention drive.

In addition, we were soon able to deliver modern data services and deploy machine learning and artificial intelligence models into the cloud: a feat that some had previously considered an absurd pipedream.

By this point, it was inspiring to see both people and technology beginning to interact with significantly less friction, and a considerable amount of data and artificial intelligence capabilities were being developed in parallel. Our speed of change – together with the speed of operational execution – was substantially increasing, and a radically different framework for enhancing value alignment had been established.

It was also clear that we were experiencing the beginnings of a successful combination of *interactional speed* and *frictionless scale* across the firm – of a kind where outcomes could be compared to a mobile phone network or the incredible workings of the human brain. Due to the strategies we deployed, our landscape was becoming more robust and resilient. Rigidity was progressively replaced by adaptability, allowing products and services to be brought online or taken offline with more ease than was previously considered achievable. At the same time, our individual silos were functioning at a higher level of *autonomy* while simultaneously achieving the *integration* that was vital for realising an ambitious vision.

Beyond that, one of my most memorable recollections was the story of Sam, the new team member who was, within a matter of hours, able to deliver results that only two years ago would have taken months to achieve. I found it even more remarkable that Sam, within a few months of joining the firm, had already gained many new cool skills and was fully embedded into our internationally dispersed teams.

Finding the appropriate intersection between *autonomy* and *integration* was vital for more than creating an empowered culture and delivering customer-facing new tech into the cloud.

Not too long ago, I had been summoned to the office of one of the group's most senior executives. She had been frustrated by having to wait over five years for critical insights from the organisation's data. She had also been concerned about the operational performance of some existing data and analytics products. The changes we had now made, and our emerging cloud-enabled data factory, were radically transforming our entire pipeline. This was enabling us to make some of our most critical legacy processes up to 30 times faster and much more resilient, despite these processes being dependent on antiquated technologies that were far beyond their sell-by dates. An example of a direct consequence of our transformation comes from one of the processes that had caused deep concern for the senior executive: the results she had to wait for over three weeks in the past were now being delivered in under three hours.

While there is no shortage of evidence of the benefits that well-functioning silos can bring to organisations, there can also be little doubt of the suboptimal implications of a poorly functioning network of silos.

So, silos can be good, and silos can be bad.

Fought between the two noble houses of the Lancasters and the Yorks, the Wars of the Roses were a series of civil wars ignited by fierce contentions for the English throne following the death of King Edward III and preceded the strong dynastic rule of the Tudors. These feuds, which inspired the award-winning *Game of Thrones* series, were additionally significant for the extent of their sheer, inescapable brutality.

While I am yet to personally witness any blood being shed in the "wars of the silos," it nevertheless reminds me of the 15th century Wars of the Roses due to the fierce arguments and entrenched positions of some of the individuals and leaders within organisations. Some have actively created silos to enable them to deliver beneficial outcomes to their firms while others openly take action aimed at breaking silos down. The resulting tensions have, over the past few decades, seen senior leaders within individual organisations at loggerheads, in effect pitting leaders, departments or even entire firms against each other.

But what if, rather than waging wars, we could achieve the best of both worlds? Could we combine becoming substantially *autonomous* while simultaneously achieving sufficient levels of *integration*? Could we foster focus and efficiency alongside adaptability and connectedness? Can we successfully enable both *interactional speed* and *frictionless scale*?

In fact, the overarching approach to connecting silos, introduced in this book, is not limited to establishing appropriate connectivity between existing silos. It is also applicable to the intentional establishment of new silos and is supportive of building them in a way that enhances their individually useful capacity while ensuring effective connectedness.

8

Reset – Interactional Scope Redefined

Early on a Monday morning, I had just settled at my desk when I heard someone call me from behind.

"Hi Ed, I'm sorry to accost you first thing, but do you have a few minutes?"

It was Ian, a project manager who oversaw some highly visible initiatives at TAG. However, the face of this typically tall, confident, even imposing figure showed an unusually worried expression.

"Thanks for resolving our resource challenge so very quickly," he said. "That was super exciting news to receive going into the weekend."

It was somewhat out of character to see him so deeply express his appreciation, in spite of a timeline that ensured resources were made available within weeks of budget approval, a turnaround that historically would have taken many months – or sometimes over a year – to achieve. Yet, the source of his look of concern, which didn't match the seemingly positive message, became evident as he continued, "But, the proposed multi-location of resources is just not the way we run projects and, I am afraid, it is not going to work."

This was the beginning of a battle that would rage for months – a battle between two stakeholder camps, a battle centred around location silos.

For the *hold-firm* camp, the goal was maintaining the status quo, it was having all resources allocated to a project under a single roof and staying location-centric. For the *demolish-all* camp, the emphasis was on sharply focused outcomes, on increasing the speed of change. Theirs was a focus on results at all costs.

There was no compromise in sight. Names were called, labels were given. The *hold-firm* camp was convinced that the *demolish-all* camp, on the one hand, was made up of a bunch of cowboys who had not thought this through and who had insufficient exposure to enterprise-scale change. The *demolish-all* camp, on the other hand, was adamant that the *hold-firm* group was limited by a self-imposed tunnel vision and stuck in a self-serving echo chamber.

A number of colleagues warned that this battle was an exercise in futility and that attempts to alter the status quo could result in career suicide.

"Many have tried before, Ed, and just as many have failed," one colleague said, genuinely concerned about the potential ramifications of what she considered "rattling the cage."

Yet, within months, it all changed.

Deeply embroiled in the depths of ideological disputes, neither camp seemed sufficiently focused on the organisational "to what end" – the successful combination of *interactional speed* with *frictionless scale*, which the firm's leadership believed was the way to fulfil its ambition of simultaneously driving growth and profitability. When we shifted our attention from biased ideological disputes to a focus on the firm's underlying purpose, the move towards crafting tangible solutions was surprisingly swift.

The world was a completely different place in the years before 2020, without Brexit or Covid-19, yet what we achieved seemed revolutionary. Our location-centric culture underwent a radical transformation into virtual engagement by default. And while the change was not driven by a global pandemic – our key lessons appear to be pertinent as today's society emerges from the pandemic.

Within months, decades-old individual and location silos were being transformed in a shift towards stronger relationships and towards a genuinely empowered *all hands collaborative culture*. This culture, in turn, enabled project delivery and operational support facilitation across multiple sites, a situation that was previously considered unthinkable.

Within months, we had initiated a move away from a deeply divisive federated model and instead adopted a *no HQ distributed team* policy, with both leaders and contributors distributed across multiple locations, a policy that was credited with enhancing not only respect and empowerment but also trust and accountability.

During this time, our focus turned away from theories and ceremonies – such as are typically associated with the "way things had always been done"; with Agile, DevOps, MLOps and DataOps or with other buzzword methodologies – and instead turned towards *visibility and flow*, providing internal transparency as well as gradually increasing confidence and integrity across all teams, all locations and all stakeholder groups.

None of these outcomes were, in theory, unprecedented. Yet, while examples of such results were well documented and studied, they rarely emerged in real-world settings and organisations. TAG, for instance, had previously invested in numerous multimillion-dollar transformation programmes promising such changes over the years, all without tangible results. Many methodologies had been implemented by name – while the firm continued to be afflicted with inertia and growing *interactional frictions*.

The main reason these efforts didn't yield a tangible impact, in my view, was not a shortage in funding but instead could be found in a collective resistance to change.

In hindsight, there was no shortage of obstacles to transformation, among them an abundance of *concealed concerns*. The presence of *concealed concerns* made a focus on the firm's purpose – the "to what end" – an essential precursor for crafting tangible solutions.

My observation of possible pathways to the resolution of such *concealed concerns* had started a few years before, during my work as a consultant at the Gaming Guru. The firm, which would become one of the world's largest online gaming companies with revenues in excess of 2 billion dollars, was already known as one of this century's most innovative companies. With products that were unrivalled across the global entertainment industry, the Gaming Guru enjoyed a largely unchallenged market dominance, with up to 80 per cent penetration in its most prominent jurisdictions.

Yet, below the outward success was an internal upheaval marked by behaviours that could only be described as "empire building, land grabs and turf wars."

Despite the near toxic atmosphere that lay beneath the surface, some individuals seemed able to steer clear of the embroilments. One of such individuals was Erasmus, an inordinately intelligent Greek Cypriot who was, at the time, the well-respected head of customer analytics with accountabilities extending to customer segmentation and behavioural modelling. Like many analytics and artificial intelligence professionals – across organisational and industry sector boundaries – he saw a lack of connected inputs as one of the most painful impediments to maximising the outcomes from such advanced capabilities.

"You know, sometimes I just sit and stare at my screen and wonder how this can be," Erasmus once told me in one of our regular meetings.

> I mean, we are meant to be an amazingly innovative company and, from the outside, we are envied by many. And why not? We attract some of the best talent. We have some of the best tools. We are reasonably cash rich. Yet, we struggle to make some of the most basic things happen.

Erasmus was right. There was no shortage of tools. Beyond the usual types of software found across firms, we had advanced tools that were ahead of most organisations. We were also in the midst of a significant public cloud transformation.

I had also witnessed tangible evidence substantiating his claims about talent. Aside from the Gaming Guru's reputation in the traditional job market, we were inundated with applications from both graduate and apprenticeships programmes.

"In theory, we don't even need to advertise job openings," a human resources manager once boasted, referring to the hundreds of competent individuals in the active pipeline he managed via LinkedIn.

Yet, when it came to our struggles with the "basics" that so frustrated Erasmus, we were not alone. Across my professional network, such complaints were commonplace, especially among well-established firms. A key challenge, recognised by data professionals across the board, was how to enable beneficial interactions between individuals who had become trapped in the silos that team structures naturally create.

"Is the solution to this madness for us to radically change our structure and the way we are organised?" Erasmus wondered.

> Maybe we should consider the kind of transformation some companies are trying, like moving from a hierarchical structure to what some call a network structure? As radical as this might be, I am actually quite happy to support something like that.

Yet, I was not convinced this would produce our desired outcomes. While such ideas typically came from highly educated and qualified management professionals, I had not seen any evidence to support their efficacy for delivering tangible, sustainable and lasting change, such as those that we so desperately needed. The effective transformations I had observed over the years had not come from lines and diagrams shown on paper or on PowerPoint slides. Instead, they have been the results of shifts in mindsets and the changes in stereotypical behaviour that such mindset shifts can drive.

To facilitate a deeper exploration of approaches to addressing this challenge, I decided to look at some fundamentals for connecting data sets.

For connecting any two or more data sets, it is essential to identify the attributes that they have in common since such attributes help to define the relationship between groups of data.

Take, for example, a retailer trying to link data about where people live to the kinds of purchases they make. To make this happen, the organisation could acquire postal code-based demographic data about their customers and combine this data set with their customers' in-store transactions. Given that such data exist in separate silos, connecting them requires identifying what they both have in common. In this case, one common attribute is the "person" data, which appears in the postal data set alongside the home address as well as the in-store transaction data about the items that have been purchased. This common "person" data point can allow retailers to bring these two data silos together to advance their understanding of potential relationships between where people live and what they buy.

Over the years, organisations across multiple industry sectors have become obsessed with collecting enriching data sets, with demographic data becoming corporate favourites. Organisations are keen to gain insights about their customers – in order to serve them better and make beneficial investment decisions. To achieve this, they collect a variety of data sets to build and extend the profiles of individual customers. Some of the most common demographic research variables typically focus on age, sex, race, income level, employment situation, location, homeownership status, levels of education, preferences, hobbies or even broader lifestyle attributes. However, just like in the example of the retailer, the challenge with integrating acquired demographic data is that they exist within silos that are separate from the customer data they are seeking to enrich. Therefore, identifying common boundary connectors is required to facilitate individual pairings.

An interesting phenomenon is that the power of the insights achievable from such pairing exercises increases significantly as additional data silos get connected and a network of data variables emerges. As firms race to find the appropriate intersection between *interactional speed* and *frictionless scale*, the allure of these powerful benefits seem a sufficient driver for pushing through projects to assemble such data networks to enhance the outcomes that can be delivered through analytics and artificial intelligence. And so, while there is no shortage of divergent opinions about data relationship strategies – for instance, the debate between surrogate key proponents and those who consider natural identities more reliable – there is absolutely no question about the importance of establishing credible links between data silos.

I have also noticed some commonalities between team silos and data silos. As is the case with data silos, it is helpful to identify commonalities for connections between disparate teams. These could include shared goals and objectives but could also extend to features like similar ways of working, shared behaviours, or shared beliefs and incentives.

As with data, it is also clear that there are exponential benefits to be gained by connecting teams and by creating the vital intersection between high *autonomy* and sufficient *integration* that allows firms to adequately address the silo paradox.

However, unlike the relative ease with which we can identify a data field that one data set might have in common with another one, identifying common attributes among individuals or teams that are sufficiently tangible and consistent for establishing a similarly mechanical connection, is much more complicated. The characteristics that teams of individuals display are more subjective than data attributes, which are factual by nature – they are a lot more qualitative than quantitative and far more ambiguous.

"How can we capture something so loosely defined, so fluid and subjective, for the purpose of enabling teams to connect and interact more seamlessly?" asked Erasmus, echoing similar big questions, which I had dedicated a significant portion of my career over the past decade, to finding the answers for.

In one of these attempts, during my consultancy engagement at the Gaming Guru, I encountered an almighty dilemma. On the one hand, there had been a growing demand for data and analytics services – and this drove a rapid expansion of teams to enable the delivery of projects at an acceptable pace. Within a few months, we grew our data capability from five teams to ten. On the other hand, to sustain such rapid growth, a strategy was chosen that meant teams would be federated across sites and countries. While we faced some constraints related to location capacity and budget, the strategy was expected to benefit from the organisation's broader pool of potential candidates.

However, this proved particularly challenging, not just because of distance or language differences but because of the inherent frictions associated with such intangibles as cultural differences and variations in labour market practices.

In the early days, there seemed an underlying sense of separation between what was perceived by some to be the "HQ" teams and the teams located in "remote sites." A number of individuals working in remote sites often seemed to view their roles as less significant, or on occasion, even inferior.

Strategies to counter these challenges were urgently devised and deployed. While such strategies sought to promote virtual and cross-location team interactions, meetings stayed decidedly one-sided. An external observer looking in could have easily made the assumption that an unwritten pact was in play, where the remote site team members non-verbally delegated authority to the HQ team members for both information provision and decision-making.

I particularly recall a personal exchange with Vlad, one of the remote site team members, after a meeting. He had remained extremely passive throughout what was otherwise a passionate debate about a new design proposition. Then, towards the end of the call, he suddenly exploded.

"Could somebody just bloody well tell us what to do?" Vlad screamed.

After a moment of stunned silence, I could almost feel a palpable sense of judgement from the others on the call. The outburst was out of character for Vlad, from whom I had never seen anything other than a calm and respectful demeanour, even in heated situations.

At the same time, it seemed to be the norm for some senior team members to employ condescending language with the expectation that those on the receiving end simply accept such utterances without challenge. Not this time.

It came as a surprise that Jim, the project manager who seemed to have triggered Vlad's reaction with both his tone and language, did not react to the outburst. Jim was not known for his humility or for being able to diffuse heated situations. In fact, rumour had it that his conduct was being closely monitored by the HR department. So, on reflection, it was unsurprising that the meeting had ended with some level of confrontation.

Yet, when I sent a text message suggesting a chat, his response – "of course, Ed" – was just as polite and respectful as I would have expected from Vlad. I was now even more convinced that there were significant *concealed concerns* hidden beneath the surface.

Some of the answers came pouring out during my conversation with Vlad.

"To be honest, Ed, I am quite ashamed of myself and regret allowing Jim to get to me like this," Vlad said. "But this situation is clearly much more than this single incident."

He described how random comments – around water coolers and coffee machines – reflected an assumed preferential treatment experienced by those in the London office.

"The other day, some of my teammates were discussing how they were not surprised that yet another cloud migration project was once again assigned to a London team," he said. "It just seems to be much more than a coincidence how only the legacy projects – that nobody in London seems to want – come to us."

Most people he talked to openly wondered why those in remote sites never seemed to get selected for the juiciest projects. He also described an atmosphere rife with an underlying divisive undercurrent, an "us" versus "them" mentality, where people perceived two camps, the "Brits" versus "the rest."

"But tell me honestly," I wanted to know. "Do you really feel that such a divide exists?"

"Yes," he responded without much hesitation. "But it's fair to say that this doesn't extend to everyone on the management team. There are those who seem more willing to work across sites, who don't show the kind of favouritism that others clearly have."

"Look, Vlad, I appreciate you being so open with me and for taking this call so late. I know it's dinnertime for you and I am grateful for your flexibility in spite of being two hours ahead of us." I signed off, asking him to leave this with me and promising to circle back within the next few days.

"Sure, Ed, and many thanks for your intervention," he replied.

Vlad's words left me in no doubt that there was genuine frustration brewing – and that only pertinent action could prevent the situation from escalating to a full-scale blow-up. I guessed that his outburst was the result of penned up frustration or even desperation.

I would later confirm that part of the trigger was that he did not feel like an empowered participant in the decision-making process despite leading a local team and that he found this perceived subordination neither desirable nor helpful.

Our follow-up conversation not only substantiated these suspicions but also sounded the alarm bells about a much broader underlying discontentedness. I suspected that there were even more *concealed concerns* that needed to be unearthed and resolved.

Over the following days and weeks, it became increasingly clear that in order to gain the benefits that this intellectually and culturally diverse group of internationally federated silos had the potential to bring, something tangible had to change. Now, the big questions were: "What could change? And what should change?"

Throughout my career, I've encountered many such stories. While each firm's setting was different – and the backdrop for the numerous situations were very varied – there were some striking similarities to the strategies that yielded the most tangible successes: they typically started with initiating an *intentional reset*.

When I first arrived at TAG, the atmosphere was far from ideal. The level of disharmony was palpable, and there was an unmistakable air of antipathy, a sense of "us" versus "them." In some cases, people refused to meet with others even within their own teams – seemingly because they had originally started in different subsidiaries of the firm or were based in different locations. In one instance, colleagues travelled to a location where some of their teammates worked. Despite spending over a week on site, neither the visiting group nor those based there made any attempt to physically meet for as much as an in-person introduction.

Morale was low. There seemed a disconnection between the doers and those who made decisions. I saw a noticeable amount of apathy and disaffection, driven by heightening levels of discontentment. Complaint levels seemed surprisingly low but so was participation in engagement opportunities, such as staff surveys. At meetings, proceedings typically started with senior leaders airing their views, followed by not much more than those same thoughts or ideas being paraphrased and regurgitated by any others who cared to speak at all.

As with most organisations where I witnessed a successful transformation, the *intentional reset* at TAG had at least two components.

The first was a focus on redefining *interactional scope*. The organisation had a transformation programme in place when I joined. There were a number of moving parts. Some business units were being reformed while others were being divested. Retained business units were also undergoing changes, with some departments expanding in size to accommodate some resultantly orphaned functions from others. Some other business units shrunk in size or disappeared altogether.

Among the most conspicuous consequences of these movements were the amalgamation of people and functional capabilities originating from various business entities and locations. There were also a number of unintended consequences.

I especially recall the nightmare situation after a failure to share vital information across our 24/7 support teams, which had resulted in our customers being detained by the police. That morning, I had been keen to get an update on my drive into work.

"The pipeline is now back up and running," said one senior team member who was based in India. "Everything is ready on *our* side but we are just waiting for *them* to move the files into staging."

This seemed like good progress since our last conference call about half an hour ago, and I was keen to get more details on tangible outcomes before my next cross-departmental management meeting. Unsure whether I had heard right – through the background noise and the poor phone connection – I sought clarification on the "them" who now needed to unblock the files.

My colleague's response pointed at members of our own data team, separated only by location, but his phrasing told me that our journey towards connecting our silos would require more than yet another set of reporting line shifts or proclamations about novel organisational principles and approaches.

The second component concerned efforts to ensure *vision clarity*. One of the key steps for TAG was the initiation and coordination of over a 100 hours of discovery sessions, engaging with more than 200 stakeholders from across multiple site locations, business units and trans-organisational functions. The consolidation of the thousands of data points that these interactions generated led to a clear articulation of our ambitions as well as our challenges and constraints. This provided valuable input for our strategy and roadmap – and helped to craft a vision that was not only clear but extensively aligned.

The situation at TAG was by no means identical to the one at the Gaming Guru. Beyond being firms from distinctly different industry sectors, there were notable differences in the levels of maturity, in scale and in size. Yet the similarity of experiences gained at both organisations point to insights that seem universally relevant. Such *intentional reset* strategies demonstrate high degrees of cross-organisational applicability.

Insights, such as these, were particularly pertinent given the urgency of closing the chasm that had evolved between teams throughout the Gaming Guru's operations. There was a desperate need to connect the silos that had formed with such detrimental consequences. There were, however, other pressing questions that had to be answered.

First, we needed to understand the attributes that both individuals and teams had in common. We needed to be clear about our interactional scope, we needed to know who among our pool of team members most embodied such common attributes, and we needed to know how a compelling vision could drive a desperately needed *interactional reset*.

9

Reverse – Peeling Back the Layers

Addressing the perceptions and beliefs – which had formed quickly and then steadily solidified – in the minds of the Gaming Guru's remote site team members had to be part of our strategy for connecting silos. Yet we knew that effective solutions depended on finding appropriate footholds – for where the bridges connecting those on either side of the gulf might be anchored. We needed to, in effect, identify the individuals who best embodied common attributes and behaviours across multiple teams. It was not sufficient to just set up a few more meetings or form yet another task force – such initiatives had been tried and had failed to deliver tangible outcomes.

To enable a radical shift towards a substantially autonomous organisational environment that was also able to deliver sufficient levels of integration, we needed more than the standard playbook that had so often been relied upon. We felt that the kind of *purposeful revelation* that open social platforms provide could enable us to achieve the combination of *interactional speed* and *frictionless scale* that was required for diffusing existing tensions – and for realising the full potential of our underlying capabilities.

This was in no way a simple or straightforward undertaking. First of all, even after some senior leaders agreed that this approach was worth trying, it was difficult to reach consensus on how to go about it. There was no shortage of ideas, some of which seemed potentially counterproductive.

"We could just create a simple survey for all remote teams," someone suggested.

"Just increasing our physical presence in remote sites should do the trick," another colleague said. "I don't think this is such a big issue, but

DOI: 10.1201/9781003278276-12

maybe we could just suggest the promotion of one of the remote team leads?"

"I think we should actually explore moving in the other direction, really centralising control, instead of having all these silos," someone insisted while another suggested that, "we should only need to send more regular management updates to remote teams."

Needless to say, the first few leadership meetings on the subject were not a roaring success. Yet I remained convinced that there were similarities between effective human connections and effective data networks.

My conviction grew when I saw positive results from some of the experimentation we were conducting from a data perspective. In a controversial departure from the traditional monolithic data model, we broke big complex structures into smaller simple ones. The idea was that by intentionally creating such simpler structures, we would gain the kind of adaptability and flexibility that loosely defined networks of data silos could achieve and that traditional monolithic structures lacked.

Yet, these successes came from the world of data. Could these approaches be applicable to human connections as well? To explore this further, I turned to Raluca, a long-time trusted collaborator, who was perfect for bouncing off such ideas since she had experience with AI, data and technology as well as a PhD in psychology with particular expertise in physical social networks.

While Raluca's views were not much different from those she had expressed in our numerous conversations about the subject of social networking, especially regarding the critical role of "boundary connectors," this time, there was something new.

"Look Ed, for me, I must stress that only a much deeper and more thoughtful approach than the situation you are currently describing is likely to move the needle for you guys," she said. She cautioned that if we looked only at the boundaries of a silo, we would potentially create an even more complex – and perhaps unadaptable – matrix organisation.

"This is an area of difference between how we might consider highly flexible data networks and how we can achieve adaptable human connections," I said.

Would you say that what we are talking about here may not be too dissimilar from the idea of the kind of connectivity in our brains? The incredible neural networks that give us our individual capabilities – and the mind-boggling synaptic connections that make our brains even more powerful than previously thought?

"Yes, absolutely," Raluca agreed.

> The trouble is that most firms really struggle to make this work, perhaps
> partly because the whole idea of a connected organisation sometimes gets
> misconstrued into the notion of 'breaking down silos.' There are some who
> believe that such an approach would lead to chaos – but, in fact, it is those
> kinds of interventions that manifest as matrix structures that actually lead
> to such chaos.

She continued,

> Some leaders jump too quickly to 'what additional processes need to be put
> in place to make this work.' What often gets missed is that making such a
> strategy work is just as much about what things firms need to get rid of. In
> some cases, what is required is a *deliberate reversal* of things we have become
> accustomed to, even in fairly young organisations or startups.

While I often considered similar thoughts in the context of some of the
tangible results I had observed, it was gratifying to hear them validated by
someone with Raluca's expertise and experience.

> With most of the data transformations I have driven over the years, a key
> goal has always been reducing the distance between parts of systems. For
> instance, a lot of data pipelines have many more steps than they need. With
> more steps between one point and another, you typically have to cover a
> greater distance, which can lead to increased friction and reduced speed,

I said. "This situation with data does in some ways sound very similar to
what we are talking about here: in terms of people and teams."

"Absolutely," Raluca responded.

It was clear that we had to explore much beyond the edges of silos,
especially if combining substantial *autonomy* with dynamic *integrations*
remained the ultimate goal. It was also helpful to look at distance reduction
for addressing interactional challenges – among people as well as in data
and artificial intelligence.

I was particularly intrigued by Raluca's insistence that the transformation
needed for achieving the vital combination of *interactional speed* and
frictionless scale was reliant on not only starting to do certain things but
also stopping some past practices.

The idea of a *deliberate reversal* reminded me of the many times when I've
seen firms – which on the surface could be considered advanced – struggle

to adapt to match the complexities and pace of change within their individual markets and across the scope of their specific commercial interests.

In the majority of these cases, leaders pinned their hopes on either a combination of new data and AI capabilities or on measures for breaking down silos as the silver bullet for achieving success. In reality, most of these situations ended up with the worst of both worlds: poorly conceived data and AI investments and costly yet cumbersome organisational structures unable to accommodate rapidly changing needs of their target customers, clients or markets.

More than ever, I was keen to get beyond paying lip service to these issues – or limiting my engagement to such initiatives as "ticking the box" of management visiting sites at the Gaming Guru – to truly getting to understand the underlying concerns and particular team characteristics. It seemed clear that none of the ideas floated by the leadership team were likely to achieve tangible outcomes. We needed to collaboratively work things through, not just with the people perceived to be in power but with the team members who were most impacted by the status quo.

And, as soon as this first step was accomplished, our focus had to shift to creating a framework for establishing necessary connections, identifying important interaction protocols and constructing effective interfaces and gateways to empower free flowing and unencumbered collaboration across silos.

In further interactions with Vlad and a group of stakeholders I had brought together, I noticed that a strong focus on hierarchies had created psychological blockers with implications that went beyond psychology.

"Do you know how long we have to wait to get design approval from our data, solutions, and enterprise architecture bosses in London?" I was once asked.

While I knew it was not a quick process, I had been unaware that this sometimes took many weeks or even months. I would later find that, ironically, such long delays were most commonly associated with projects that were considered relatively low priority, such as the legacy initiatives typically assigned to remote teams.

I was convinced that addressing *interactional frictions* would not only help to connect our silos but would also create significant efficiencies across the board.

An example of an initiative that targeted such hierarchies and sought to limit such bottlenecks was the adaptation of the firm's data design clinic.

Data design clinics were not new to the Gaming Guru – they were among the many practices the firm had evolved by adapting agile methodologies. In their original incarnation, design clinics primarily served as a closed forum where local engineering teams met to brainstorm ideas. The ideas generated in these sessions could then lead to the production of a design proposal, which the engineering teams would bring to an architecture review board for scrutiny – and eventual authorisation.

In this model, the workflow was hampered by unhelpful *interactional frictions*, which also impeded *interactional speed*. Aside from the obvious bottlenecks that could delay the implementation of ideas, the practice also imposed an implicit layer of hierarchy between the functions of engineering and architecture. This was not captured on any of the firm's organisational charts, however, the unilateral authority assigned to the architecture teams insinuated a level of hierarchical supremacy over their engineering colleagues, leading to an unintended unhealthy combination of inertia and resentment.

In a subsequent adaptation of the process, design responsibilities were assumed by the engineering teams, which meant they could now advance the design of their products and services without the bottleneck of an architecture review. This provided enhanced *autonomy* to the engineering teams and delivered instant boosts to the ambition of reducing *interactional friction* while increasing *interactional speed*.

The new format allowed design clinics to transition to becoming open forums for richer multifunctional and multilocational collaborations, with inputs from architecture, security, governance, platforms and operations teams across sites.

In this new incarnation, the focus had shifted away from structures and hierarchies and towards purpose, the ultimate "to what end" and a *deliberate reversal* of the way things had previously been done.

While this model had shown good results, I also wanted to explore some of the other ideas proposed by the leadership team.

"Do you think it would help if managers and senior leaders visited sites more regularly?" I asked.

Vlad's response was respectful but candid. "Some people enjoy the duty free chocolates and sweets that managers bring us when they visit," he said. "But to be fair, many of my colleagues don't have the impression that senior managers genuinely make the effort to try to really understand them."

So the visits were not seen as a bad thing, but the level of engagement was clearly perceived as lacking. I also found it interesting that there was no mention of quantity: the number and frequency of visits were not front of mind for the teams outside London.

However, it was clear that if such visits became effective – for getting to understand the teams and individual cultures in those sites – they could be powerful tools for improving the interfaces between silos.

In our conversations, Vlad emphasised that what most remote team members craved was not to be talked at or provided regurgitated updates that were typically available through a variety of channels but to be listened to. Instead of bringing chocolates and sweets, they wanted visitors to be sufficiently open to observing and experiencing their cultural realities. Rather than being considered "remote," they wanted to be part of an integrated system of teams. It turns out that what they all wanted was much simpler than many assumed: equity.

In order to achieve this, another *deliberate reversal* – of the way interactional relations were organised – seemed to be required. This was by no means a trivial undertaking. Firstly, the individuals involved had to be willing to commit to changing the way of doing things to which they had become accustomed. However, the challenge of achieving the required level of commitment paled in comparison to the nuances and complexities associated with two other important areas we needed to address.

Secondly, it was clear that there could be language challenges and things lost in translation, particularly where multiple nationalities were involved. I had encountered similar challenges in the past: one of these was in the course of my work on an E.U. wide transformation for a European multilateral organisation.

On a Friday morning, near the end of our usual team meeting, a Bulgarian colleague asked if we would all be able to meet for drinks later that evening. Though most team members said yes, I told them I would unfortunately not be able to join.

"I am afraid I can't make it," I said. "I have some guests flying in from Australia." I was quite surprised to notice looks of concern on some of the faces around the table.

"Why are you afraid," my Bulgarian colleague asked with a frown.

I had not considered that such an expression might not be understood in this setting. I explained that rather than being "afraid" in a literal sense, this was an idiomatic expression I was accustomed to using when I had to decline an invitation or answer a question in the negative.

"I suppose it is meant to indicate regret that I have to say 'no' to something I would have preferred to say 'yes' to," I said.

The frowns around the table turned to laughter and relief as I reflected on how easily things can get lost in translation.

The third – and perhaps most challenging – was where a targeted *deliberate reversal* was essential for addressing the kinds of clashes of cultures I have found across numerous organisations and across industry sectors. The situation at the European multilateral organisation offered a good example of such a clash, where interactional relations were at an all-time low and a radical mindset shift was required. Much like the Gaming Guru, the European multilateral organisation's multicultural teams were located in sites spread across a number of European cities.

In one remarkable incident, I was sitting in a meeting room with eight other colleagues: one Icelandic, one Italian, two Finns, a Bulgarian, a German, a Swede and a Spaniard. Jukka, one of the Finns, was a well-respected subject matter expert who regularly contributed to one of my projects. The meeting had been in progress for about 45 minutes, and our exchanges seemed to be going nowhere.

The typically reserved Jukka had been even quieter than usual when a loud series of bangs suddenly interrupted the proceedings. It was Jukka.

"Will somebody make a decision or are we going to keep sitting here to play ping pong until lunchtime," he yelled.

This perplexing outburst brought a flashback of a recent conversation. I had been in the canteen having lunch with a few colleagues when somebody brought up the topic of cultural differences among Europeans.

"Consider the Swedes and the Finns, who are neighbouring nations with histories tightly intertwined for many centuries. Yet, they could not be more different when it comes to meetings," said a Danish colleague.

> I remember working for this company that was part Finnish and part Swedish. When it came to decision-making, the Swedes were very democratic. They would get everyone involved, have lots of coffee conversations, and would shy away from any decisions that were at risk of not finding consensus. The Finns, on the other hand, were very pragmatic and would prefer to quickly make a decision, even at risk of some contention. You know, there is this proverb 'speech is silver but silence is golden.' I remember someone saying that Finns take this quite literally.

Despite the challenges, we saw some notable changes in our drive towards a *deliberate reversal* of our legacy ways of interacting within a couple of months of making the commitment. And soon after, tangible outcomes were reflected in our staff surveys. Yet it was clear that more could be done to accelerate this transformation and to enhance the connections between our silos. An additional intervention I was keen to test was the "No HQ" strategy I had previously employed with notable results.

At TAG, this strategy enabled us to move away from a deeply divisive federated model towards a *no HQ, distributed team* model, with both leaders and contributors present across multiple locations. In this situation, the shift had enhanced respect as well as leading to higher levels of empowerment, trust and accountability across broadly dispersed locations.

Some of its implementation had been relatively simple: at its core, it involved the non-preferential rotation of hosting locations for cross-functional team meetings and other activities.

"But isn't this just going to be logistically challenging, especially for those who lead or initiate such meetings or activities?" a skeptic wanted to know.

I agreed that this would be the case if leaders had to take sole responsibility for such implementation. However, the model presented a real opportunity for empowering both teams and individuals.

"Would you think many would be opposed to actually empowering individuals within sites to rotationally take responsibility for hosting such events?" I asked.

The outcomes were phenomenal. Beyond a radical shift in atmosphere, which such empowerment seems to instantaneously deliver, the gatherings progressively turned into popular "all hands" participatory events. Unlike meetings where leaders present information to a passive audience, ours saw increasing engagement across teams, where empowered individuals from different sites took ownership of the events and effectively circumvented pre-existing *interactional frictions*.

Another pathway I wanted to explore was the virtualisation of projects. Aside from the benefits that cross-locational collaboration would bring for connecting silos, a big selling point was the additional flexibility this would enable for combining disparate skills. Too often, we had faced situations where single locations did not have all the required skills or resources to fully deliver one project. However, if we could combine the talent and resources from multiple sites, such challenges would be significantly reduced.

Similar to my experience at TAG, virtual projects were not standard practice at the Gaming Guru as neither the appropriate structures nor tooling had been put in place. There was also some resistance to moving to such a model, since being in close physical proximity to project teams was considered an essential ingredient for success.

I remembered the arguments about location silos for a few challenging months at TAG, when we were embroiled in a battle between two camps.

For the *hold-firm* camp, on the one hand, it was all about maintaining the status quo, about having all resources allocated to projects under a single roof, about remaining location-centric. The *demolish-all* camp, on the other hand, was focused on outcomes, on increasing the speed of change and on achieving results at all cost.

There had seemed to be no compromise in sight. Names were called, labels given. The *hold-firm* camp was convinced that the *demolish-all* camp was made up of a bunch of cowboys, who had not thought this through and who had insufficient exposure to enterprise scale change. The *demolish-all* camp was adamant that the *hold-firm* group was limited by a self-imposed tunnel vision and stuck in a self-promoting echo chamber.

It was a battle that many saw as an exercise in futility. Yet by shifting our attention from biased ideological disputes to a focus on the firm's underlying purpose, the "unwinnable battle" was swiftly resolved, and it had all changed in a matter of months.

At the Gaming Guru, it was clear that a rapid transition was already in motion. While the fabric of the teams and underlying capabilities that had been built over the years remain sound, the *interactional frictions* that impeded our desire to achieve *frictionless scale* were melting away. Staff morale was up, and there was a sense of empowered alignment across silos, which would have been difficult to imagine only months ago. The combined effects of our interventions and the *deliberate reversal* of the unhelpful elements in our legacy ways of interacting had relegated the notion of "remote sites" to the firm's historical archives.

Yet I was convinced that empowerment could be further improved. I had seen positive impacts from efforts to intentionally create safe spaces for frictionless decision-making and wanted to encourage the creation of such an environment.

One particular comment from an experienced team member at TAG came to mind. Her name was Fatima, and she had joined the firm two years before my arrival. On one occasion, I asked for feedback about the progress of our transformation. In her positive response, she went so far as to suggest that "it was way beyond" any of her expectations. She also admitted that she sometimes felt "over empowered."

What made her response particularly meaningful was that it came from an individual who had previously agonised over a lack of empowerment and responsibility.

I realised that when it came to empowerment, our key challenges were connected to boundaries, which could be either too restrictive or too ambiguous. A senior leader once confirmed this idea. He said his organisation intentionally left boundaries vague in order to "break down silos and to force people to collaborate."

While the intention was credible, one unfortunate outcome was that this often had the opposite effect. Rather than extending their scope, lots of people limited their actions and decision-making instead. In some situations, this reluctance to act was driven by the fear of inadvertent encroachment. In other cases, both parties might assume that specific tasks would be the other's responsibility, opening wide the risk of items potentially falling through the cracks.

At first glance, this seemed counterintuitive. Yet we later confirmed that contrary to conventional wisdom, boundaries didn't restrict individuals or teams. Instead, they served to empower them. We also found that the clearer the boundaries, the greater the sense of accountability – and the safer people felt in making decisions. These insights inspired us to define boundaries in such a way that individuals or teams could make their own decisions. By giving individuals more generous boundaries, we were providing them with more freedom to act.

My journey to address these challenges at the Gaming Guru also reminded me of a previous experience during a consultative engagement with one of the largest multilateral organisations in Europe. Here, the vision was to improve safety and standards by imposing regulations, which were described as the most complex in European history, as well as reducing regulatory overheads by a radical decentralisation of accountability. As with many such undertakings, success or failure was inextricably linked to data.

The project's core strategy was particularly innovative: create a platform for enabling manufacturers, importers and transporters of products within this regulatory domain to interact and identify divergence in standards, often induced or exacerbated by poor data quality. While this platform had the capability to identify correlations between complex product structures – sometimes forging links between hundreds of organisations that never had any previous interactions – it did not have the power to sufficiently incentivise action. The real power was in the public dissemination of information about inconsistencies in products by various brands entering the market, which left some convinced it was an intentional "name and shame" strategy. This seemed to fuel the drive for desirable action: for organisations bringing products on these markets to leverage the associated secure information exchange platform to join forces and resolve critical challenges.

I recall a meeting with the projects and legal teams, aimed at resolving some of the ambiguity within the legislative text in sections about regulations and prioritisation challenges.

"This is a difficult decision," the programme director solemnly declared. "We must present a recommendation on whether the information exchange platform can be delivered without compromising the deliverables already committed to the global press."

We recommended that it was essential that the information exchange platform should not be dropped. In hindsight, given its critical role for connecting the silos that were the individual market participants and delivering associated positive outcomes, it was indeed the most appropriate call.

Over the years, the *deliberate reversal* measures I have initiated have resulted in environments analogous to open social platforms, which provided significant positive implications for our ability to deliver tangible value while maintaining a conducive work environment. The reductions in *interactional frictions* were notable and the journeys towards *frictionless scale* significantly advanced. At their core, these measures were focused on enabling a substantially *autonomous* world, which was simultaneously able to deliver sufficient levels of *integration*, but they also brought unintended positive consequences. Indeed, some additional benefits of the increased visibility that they delivered were notable enhancements in the levels of transparency, trust and accountability.

10

Reward – Empowering Flow

Strong results showed that creating appropriate gateways and access pathways was helping to connect silos, and *deliberate reversal* measures were facilitating environments analogous to open social platforms. However, it soon became obvious that enabling spaces, establishing forums and setting up meetings would not be sufficient for achieving optimal outcomes. More had to be done to create impetus – to accelerate shifts in cultural norms, to make it desirable to chart this new path with the level of urgency that was essential for successfully connecting silos.

The key questions now were: how can we generate sufficient buy-in? And how can we create effective incentives to drive appropriate action?

At certain points during my past experiences, some approaches had resulted in favourable outcomes while others had not, leaving me with the conviction that past learnings could allow us to craft similar workable solutions.

Yet the idea for one practical solution implemented at TAG started from a desperate place of absolute despair.

Our transformation had been ongoing for a while at the time and while there were very clear signs of the significant progress that was being made, there was also ample evidence that all was yet to be resolved. A recent feedback note received from a demanding stakeholder seemed to aptly summarise where we seemed to be:

> You made us as your customer feel at ease, clearly articulating the new data and technology approaches we were progressing: in the cloud. It is, however, pretty clear that we still have a long way to go to get TAG's IT resolved: we appear to be a long way behind where we need to be. Although the issues pertaining to Finance - and your other key stakeholders - can be captured by you and processes can be redesigned, it is clear that many of the current idiosyncrasies are outside of your direct control.

DOI: 10.1201/9781003278276-13

It was a difficult message but one that seemed both balanced and fair. It was the kind of message that injected the kind of fuel required to drive forward with increased determination but was in stark contrast from the composition of the message I was to receive less than 24 hours later.

The energy-sapping situation was – on the surface – no more than a line item during a regular check-in meeting with my senior executive line manager, but I had significant concerns about its potentially severe ramifications.

It was information that another one of my team's end of year performance grading had been blocked. It was not the first such situation but this time it was of immense significance – as, in spite of being one of our top performers and a big driver for our transformation, her efforts were almost certain to go unrewarded because her name had been found to be listed in the notorious secret black book famously maintained by a feared and powerful senior executive.

"How could something so potentially damaging to the team and to our transformation be happening?" I remember thinking. "How badly might this damage morale, perhaps even lead to a resource exodus and a potential derailment of our increasingly successful transformation?"

I knew just where I had to turn – I knew I wanted to explore the situation with Raluca, who is not only a fountain of knowledge in the unusual combination of AI, data, technology and human psychology but had over the years proved to be one of my most trusted advisers. As a long-time trusted collaborator, she was perfect for bouncing off such ideas, and I had over the years taken advantage of her expertise – especially as this extends to the intricacies of human social networks.

Our conversation was as open as ever, and she was in agreement that this was a particularly delicate situation. "Well, I think we can both agree that if not creatively handled, this would almost inevitably lead to the unpicking of a lot of the good results you have so far achieved," she said.

Yet, rather than an expected brainstorm to come up with ideas to address the current situation, Raluca seemed keen to delve deeper. "Tell me about what has really been going on under the covers. How is the transformation - really - progressing: I would be particularly interested in the people side; the culture side of things," she asked.

I thought it best to take her back to that nightmare wake-up call. I described the drive into the office that next morning. "It was a rainy day with traffic from hell, and an overnight failure of the deployment of a critical operational service had meant very little sleep," I recalled.

I recounted how I got into the car after a flurry of early morning calls and while I was confident that steps towards resolving the situation were underway, I wanted a quick update from my colleagues who were monitoring the progress.

I recall the heavy downpour lashing my windscreen and the squeaky sound of wiper blades trying to clear the view, making it challenging to understand the voice coming through my car's hands-free speakerphone.

"Hi Ravi. Edosa here," I said. "What's the current status?"

"Hello Sir," he said, ignoring my previous attempts of encouraging him to address me by my first name. "The pipeline is now back up and running and the scheduled processes are now ready to be kicked, but we are waiting for them to move the files across to staging."

I explained how while I thought that was good progress, my focus immediately went to the word "them," which described colleagues within our own data team, separated only by location.

"That, indeed, seemed a subtle cue that all was not well," she agreed. I explained how something that would perhaps be considered quite trivial and almost certainly overlooked by most sent a strong signal that our journey towards connected silos had yet to arrive at desirable outcomes, which included reduced *interactional frictions*.

We had progressively applied numerous *deliberate reversal* measures in the preceding weeks and months, but the open and empowered environments that these measures had enabled did not automatically guarantee participation and cooperation.

Through our subsequent brainstorm, two things became clear. It was evident that in order to create a tangible shift in our mindsets and cultures, we needed to achieve alignment on why this shift was important – on our collective purpose.

Through a focus on redefining our *interactional scope* and by advancing *vision clarity*, we began to see compelling outcomes. There was ample evidence that these shifts were helping to drive a desperately needed *interactional reset*.

However, we also knew that for all these efforts to work, we needed to find tangible ways to build trust and create safe environments where collective learning and empowered creativity could become the norm.

I was especially impressed by the commitment and dedication of my team, which delivered numerous ideas in brainstorming sessions. Three proposals stood out for delivering tangible and successful outcomes.

First, there was our newly crafted "all hands" event that brought together over a 100 individuals from seven cities and three time zones. I learned that this was not only the first time my entire team – and everyone working within data – had ever come together, but the event was the first of its kind across the entire organisation. Aside from the symbolic significance of the inaugural event, its "all hands" model made it the perfect setting for the chosen theme: collaboration.

> "I have never felt such a strong connection to my colleagues."
> "The work that I do suddenly gained tangible meaning."
> "I actually had no idea how diverse we were as a department."
> "It felt so strange to realise how many people I had worked with for years but never even met."
> "Today, I learnt so much about what we actually do."
> "These were the best eight hours for a very long time."

Along with heartfelt "thank you" notes, these were among the many comments that came pouring in after the event, leaving no doubt that something shifted that day.

A notable hit was a conversation about Professor Muir's Super Chicken experiment, which was made popular by Margaret Heffernan's TED talk.

We discussed the biological experiment, which was originally intended to seek a way to improve egg-laying productivity. It started with the establishment of two groups. The base group was made up of average chickens – to observe a population where there was minimal distinction between one chicken and another. The other group had two main functions: to act as a destination for any individuals from the average chickens' group that demonstrated attributes of excellence, superiority or other extreme differentiation as well as identify and observe the highest performer or "Super Chicken." The surprise revelation was that, after six generations, the super flock had been outperformed by the average chickens. What was perhaps even more shocking was the fact that many of the super chickens had pecked their fellow members of the super flock to death.

This resonated with most of the attendees of our event – and generated a genuine vibe of solidarity and wind of change. Yet we knew it would take more than a symbolic event – and more than a bonding over killer chickens – to create the seismic shift our situation required.

The second proposal involved a shift from our legacy Root Cause Analysis (RCA) regime to an approach that focused on the Lessons Learned as a Practice (LLaaP). Aside from the shift in naming – and the fresh energy such a rebranding inherently injects – the most significant difference was that the new LLaaP approach was not compulsory and was unsupervised. For immediate and timely resolution of any operational issues, this meant participants could work out what went wrong, why it went wrong and what lessons could be captured for future application. Much of its success came from the fact that authority was shifted away from senior management figures, which was especially useful given the current level of distrust felt across teams.

Beyond its broader implications for rebuilding trust and transforming organisational culture, one comment best illustrated an important benefit: "Now, we don't have to make the same mistakes our colleagues made in order to benefit from the lessons we can learn from their experiences." This was achieved because the LLaaP framework allowed not only the capturing but also the sharing of learnt lessons.

The biggest challenge with creating an open culture – which required a high level of exposure – was how such a shift could be incentivised. It was clear that targeted incentives were needed – and this was the key focus of the third proposal, suggesting a complete overhaul of key performance indicators (KPIs).

From the simple idea, that incentives and behaviours are inextricably linked, we reviewed our legacy KPIs. It soon became obvious, that "superstardom" was inadvertently being highly incentivised and rewarded while incentives for promoting a safe environment that encourages openness, collaboration and the sharing of organisational knowledge were conspicuously absent.

"But I can't see what the problem is," one of the senior leaders in my team admitted. "We already have quite an extensive performance and rewards practice."

These practices, however, had evidently failed to sufficiently incentivise the kinds of behaviours required for reducing *interactional frictions* and for enhancing our drive towards *frictionless scale*.

We agreed that a critical assessment of our current goal setting and performance appraisal approach would be helpful, and the experience that followed was eye-opening.

One memory from that process has remained particularly vivid. During a brainstorming session about some of our engineering practices, we discussed a disturbing trend, where a progressive increase in code bugs had been leading to issues in our production systems.

"Nothing seems to be helping," an engineering team leader called Hugo complained. He was concerned that the errors in our code would reflect negatively not only on our team but also on the quality of the organisation's value proposition more broadly.

"We have improved our coding standards and made sure every engineer is aware of them. Our enhanced design clinics have been great, and we ensure that all engineers attend them," he said.

> And we have continued to call out code bugs as a specific key performance indicator and this has also been on our new dashboard. I am at a loss for why none of these seem to be helping. Instead, things seem to be taking a turn for the worse.

Hugo was right. We had done everything the textbooks said. We had implemented everything the methodologists, the human resource and HR guides recommended. Everything that seemed logical had been done, yet these steps had proved insufficient.

"It sometimes feels like I am peddling at a thousand revolutions per second but not getting very far. In some respects, it feels like we're moving backwards," he said. "If I can be honest, I often feel so frustrated that I have frankly contemplated giving up on trying."

Hugo's comments were difficult to take since we had been trying very hard without making much headway in this area. Without a course correction, we clearly faced the risk of an almighty derailment of our vision and the dire implications that would bring.

We were no experts in human behaviour or psychology, so I proposed an approach that I had found effective in the past: going back to basics, back to the "to what end." We asked ourselves,

> What are the key performance indicators that best reflect what we're trying to achieve? What is the fundamental purpose of each KPI? Why is it being captured? What change would we want it to drive? And, would capturing and publishing each of these KPIs help us deliver our desired results?

Firstly, we understood that our strategy for advancing the goals of reducing *interactional friction* and driving towards *frictionless scale* had to be underpinned by incentivising openness, increasing visibility and fostering transparency. Secondly, we wanted to improve trust and integrity by increasing code quality and reducing errors and bugs.

However, evidence suggested that the capture and publication of KPIs, which focused on reducing the number of errors and bugs, had not delivered desired outcomes for improved openness and increased code quality.

Since the number of code errors being captured through testing seemed to be on a downward trend yet issues in our live environment were increasing, I wondered whether the publication of code bug counts had caused reduced identification or disclosure from the engineering teams.

Behavioural game theorists propose that when individuals, who such theorists refer to as players, look to make decisions, they first contemplate what others are likely to do. This is typically done by going through iterations of guesses. Game theory proposes a general framework for understanding the decisions that players make in uncertain situations when payoffs are dependent on the actions taken by other players.

It was conceivable that our code bug KPI acted as a disincentive for the openness it was intended to drive among engineers and engineering teams. Bugs were either being missed or deliberately ignored due to a perceived negative impact on reputational or performance ratings.

Game theory can provide a helpful framework for understanding behaviour in interactive decision-making scenarios. When individuals and firms are better able to analyse and accurately predict likely implications of real-world situations, their mechanisms and interventions are going to be more effective.

One type of game described by the theory is the "zero-sum" game, where one player's win comes at the expense of another. The more one player gets, the more the other player must concede.

A good example of this concept comes from British football or soccer. Every goal a team scores in a football match is directly detrimental to the other team. For instance, a score of three-nil implies a three-goal lead for one team and a deficit of an equivalent proportion to the other team. If the losing team landed a goal to bring the score to three–one, the winning team's advantage is reduced to two goals. Every goal scored by a team is effectively taken out of the other team's total, creating a perpetual "win-lose" situation.

Another example comes from house pricing in a property market. Assuming a house is put on sale at an initial asking price of $100,000. If a potential buyer is able to negotiate a lower price of $90,000, then the seller stands to lose $10,000 while the buyer stands to gain $10,000. Such price negotiations are zero-sum games: the gains of one player result in equivalent losses for the other.

Much like such zero-sum games, which encourage competitive behaviour, our focus on code bugs reporting seemed to be incentivising a "win-lose" situation, with the number of code bugs declared taking away from a "score" in performance, reputation and credibility. The perception was that the more code bugs were posted on the new KPI dashboard against an individual or a team, the less performance, reputational or credibility scores were earned – that more of one element resulted in the loss of another.

That meant this intervention was causing the opposite of the intended outcomes. From asking, "What is this key performance indicator trying to achieve?" we needed to explore the question, "What interventions can help us improve trust and integrity as well as increase code quality by limiting errors and reducing bugs?"

Game theory also describes a number of non-zero-sum games. Team sports, such as football, can again offer tangible analogies. However, in contrast to the focus on the interaction between one team and another which we previously explored for the "zero-sum" game, our focus here is directed internally: to explore the internal interactions within a single team. For a football team, for instance, it is a "positive-sum" if one's team wins since that means all individual members of such a winning team have one thing in common: they all win. In such game scenarios, no one team member wins at the expense of the other, instead, everyone benefits from their collective efforts. Unlike the competitive structure of a "zero-sum" game, a "positive-sum" game is cooperative and is the sort of game some refer to as being based on solidarity.

Perhaps the most famous example of such games is the prisoner's dilemma. It invites us to imagine two people, say Jide and Juliet, who had been arrested on suspicion of robbing a local wine store and being held in separate cells. However, the challenge for the authorities is that they have no witnesses aside from the two apprehended suspects. The only way the police can gain sufficient evidence and build a case against the suspects is to convince at least one of them to betray his or her accomplice. Sensing that Jide and Juliet would care more about their individual welfare than about the other's freedom, a clever detective presented each of them with an intelligently crafted offer.

> You have two choices: stay silent or make a confession. If you choose to remain silent and your suspected accomplice confesses, then they will be freed while the evidence they provide against you could lead to a three-year jail term for you,

he said. "If instead you choose to confess and the other suspect does not, all charges against you will be dropped and the testimony that you provide will be used to secure the conviction of your suspected co-conspirator."

The detective's offer did, however, come with additional conditions.

On the other hand, if you both confess, then you would both be potentially convicted as you would both have provided evidence against each other. You would undoubtedly end up with reduced sentences of no more than two years each,

he said.

Lastly, if you both choose to stay silent, then the limited evidence that we currently have against you would mean that you both end up with a maximum of a year in prison each. The choice is entirely yours. I will, of course, be putting this same offer in front of the other suspect.

This dilemma is particularly intriguing because it pitches the interests of the individual against those of the collective. From an individual's perspective, the most self-serving choice would be to confess, which would lead to an acquittal if the other suspect stays silent. Either Jide or Juliet could also be tempted to stay silent as the next best choice since this has the potential of resulting in a token sentence of one year in jail.

While a strategy where neither confesses has the most favourable outcome for both, it could lead to a three-year prison term for one of them if the other party chose to provide evidence. With both suspects remaining in isolation until their decisions are made to ensure they cannot know the other's chosen strategy and without certainty that the other will not confess, they are both likely to confess and receive a two-year jail term.

The paradox of the prisoner's dilemma offers insights into how cooperation can create favourable outcomes for all parties. If both suspects cooperate in silence, they can minimise their total jail term to two years. However, the lack of visibility and coordination would most likely drive both of them to confess – and actually end up serving the maximum jail term of a total of four years between the two of them. According to the Nash equilibrium, a decision-making theorem within game theory, both players are likely to make the move that seems safest for them individually but worse for the collective.

There was no doubt that our transformation at TAG needed to bring us closer to a reality resembling a positive-sum game – to a day-to-day environment that supported and promoted collective success.

From a perceived hierarchical order and ensuing competition – where a fear of failure led to a lack of disclosure – we had to create the right incentives for cooperative progression. As we asked ourselves difficult questions about the core of our collective purpose, a few pathways became apparent. They included measures for increasing code quality and reducing error rates, such as testing, peer reviews, design clinic participation, design pattern reuse, code reviews and increasing automation.

It was also interesting to see that – unlike the negative correlation between the capture of error counts and our intended outcomes – measurements in these new focus areas positively correlated with our collective purpose. In other words, the more test activations, peer reviews, design clinic participation, design pattern reuse, code reviews and increasing automation we observed, the more performance, reputational or credibility scores were earned.

As with the prisoner's dilemma, we saw that a favourable collective outcome not only required *cooperation* but *visibility* as well.

Before long, the comprehensive rethink of "how do we need to reposition the use of KPIs to deliver intended outcomes?" had underpinned a complete overhaul of our approach to rewards and was already starting to yield effective incentives, through creative interventions, which had begun to accelerate our drive towards desired behaviours. Yet, our most powerful intervention was to come from an unlikely source.

During one of my remote team site visits, I was on my way back to my hotel room on a cold night. The outside world felt eerily silent, with clouds as dark as soot deepening the shadows of the deserted streets. It was my first taste of fresh air that day and my hotel was only 15 minutes away, but spears of rain – driven by bitter winds – made me momentarily miss the shelter of the bland office I had just left behind.

The brisk walk left me breathing so hard that I barely noticed my phone vibrating a few steps away from the hotel. When I fished it from my pocket with freezing fingers, I saw that the caller was Eki, a member of my data leadership team.

"Hi Eki," I said. "What's keeping you up so late? Is everything OK?"

Eki told me that our colleague Fatima had suddenly become unwell and had been rushed to the hospital.

"But she is in good hands," Eki tried to reassure me. "Everything is going to be alright."

After asking all the necessary questions, I also wanted to acknowledge Eki's kind and selfless gesture. She had hurried out the door to accompany her colleague to the hospital and was now at risk of missing a significant family engagement.

"I have no intention of leaving Fatima until she is fine," Eki asserted.

After a candid exchange – and after telling her that she was neither obliged nor expected to stay there – I felt compelled to add, "Look, Eki. Can I just say how incredibly generous this is, showing support for a colleague, especially when it upsets your personal plans."

"She is not just a colleague anymore, Edosa," Eki responded. "Fatima is now a friend."

This comment, more than anything, caused me to re-evaluate my previous assumptions about our culture, especially since I saw it not as an isolated example of two individuals taking a liking to each other but as a sign that our team's way of interacting had changed.

I don't recall the precise point when the radical shift occurred, but as I went to my hotel room that night, I pondered the "before" and "after" slices of time. If one was the "night before" and the other the "morning after," an overnight spell seemed to have teleported us from a finger-pointing "them" culture, to a team-embracing "us" culture.

I vividly recalled the blame games – and one specific conversation from the not-too-distant past that was reflective of the situation. Soon after I had come in to run the department, a new team member who reported directly to me had raised a concern.

"Would you believe that some of the team travelled to my location yesterday and did not even so much as stop by to say hello?" she had lamented, reflecting on the sad reality that members of our team did not see eye to eye in those early days.

But now I wondered how this extraordinary transformation would align with traditionally held thoughts about culture.

On the one hand, there were observers who were convinced that the cultural transformation was nothing more than happenstance. They did not believe that these changes were the results of any of the measures we implemented.

On the other hand, others had no doubt that the outcomes were directly connected to our efforts for preparing a fertile ground where such a cultural shift could take root.

"What school of thought was right?" I wondered. "Or are these differences only a matter of perspective?"

The answers to these questions might help to inform our *path to resolution*. Should we actively – and intentionally – try to influence a shift in team culture? Or should we sit back as observers in anticipation of further positive outcomes?

The changing language – from "they" to "we," from "them" to "us" and "their" to "our" – indicated a powerful shift in ownership and accountability across silos and historical boundaries.

No more finger-pointing described like this: "The service was disrupted because one of *their* processes failed" or "We will keep you updated about when *they* fix *their* problems."

Now, responses would be framed from the perspective of the collective.

"The service disruption happened because one of *our* processes failed."

"We will keep you updated and let you know when *our* fixes have been applied."

I had no doubt that we had discovered the power of pronouns – a power that would, over time, help us to tackle one of the most fundamental challenges for the scourge of cross silo *interactional friction*: voice.

Verbalised from the source, digitally codified or transformed into other means of expression, voice is the medium that transports both vital information and essential ideas across silo boundaries and through the structure of the pathways that underpin organisations.

With a solid foundation for empowering voice, the thoughts, ideas, strategies and solutions of the collective can be communicated and combined without friction through both physical and digital interactions – and transmitted across silos. And the power of pronouns will help to ensure an effective inclusion of a diversity of minds. Empowering voice additionally ensures that essential feedback loops flow unencumbered, allowing timely course corrections to be implemented and market opportunities expediently appropriated throughout the firm.

While the examples in this chapter are unique, I have found the same patterns of experience repeated from one interaction to another and from one organisation to the other.

The interventions that yielded the best results were underpinned by a focus on gaining alignment on the "to what end," on shifting from the typical zero-sum game to sustainable cooperative interactions and on crafting the most effective incentives for promoting collective action.

As these journeys illustrate, I have taken careful note of these core principles – and the results they achieved in a variety of scenarios – with the hope to contribute to the understanding of the silo conundrum and present solutions for successfully enhancing synaptic connections across silos.

Part IV

Bringing It All Together

Exposing Recombinant Evolutions of Technical Solutions and Their Practical Applications

11

Approaching a Cliff's Edge

It was a year of numerous exciting challenges that included swapping the dark winters of Helsinki for a future in London. In my personal life, it was the year of our first pregnancy and the excitement of the first skin-to-skin embrace with my first child. Over the same period, we had undertaken a mammoth home-building project fuelled by the ambition to not just to build one but two separate dwellings.

As momentous as they were, none of these milestones could sufficiently prepare me for the challenge of driving what some considered "an existential transformation" at the Gaming Guru, one of this century's most innovative companies in the global entertainment industry.

My involvement began when the company – like Netflix, LinkedIn or even Amazon – had become a victim of its own success and was at the brink of hitting painful barriers in its own effort to scale. While business demand was growing and customer numbers were swelling, its well-tuned platforms were creaking at the seams – and fast approaching a cliff's edge.

The risks were substantial, especially since the Gaming Guru considered customers' experience paramount. Since the company was struggling to scale its underlying technology infrastructure, the level of service that could be offered to customers was gradually degrading. For example, it took longer for webpages to respond to customer requests and less-than-optimal sluggishness was also creeping into mobile experience offerings.

Due to the need to adapt to increasingly complex systems, it also became more and more challenging to keep up with the demand for the development of new features, which would then increase operational pressure on already ageing platforms.

An increasingly fragmented flow of information also brought implications for the firm's ability to sufficiently address customer needs and take advantage of emerging market opportunities.

DOI: 10.1201/9781003278276-15

There was little doubt about the extent of the painful challenges we now had to contend with – and with them came big questions. For example, how do you migrate a platform underpinning an entire firm without causing noticeable disruption to its 24/7 business and customers? How do you make sense of incomprehensible dependencies across a data and analytics platform that ingested hundreds of thousands of data points in real time? How do you reimagine a complex data platform with highly complicated code bases built organically (and without supporting documentation) over many years? And how do you achieve a sizable transformation from an on-premise infrastructure to the public cloud at an acceptable speed while adhering to stringent data security requirements?

In some ways, this felt potentially more complex than replacing critically defective parts of an aircraft in mid-flight.

There was no doubt that the stakes were high. One senior executive declared that the risks were "literally existential."

Yet in hindsight, it was quite impressive how well the legacy technology infrastructure had managed to cope with exponential growth up to that point. It was clearly a testament to the group of talented engineers and digital and data specialists whom the organisation had managed to attract. I recall talking to at least two platform vendors who were in awe of the inventiveness that had been applied to extend their platforms' capabilities.

Creativity seemed to flow naturally through the organisation's veins, with innovation embedded in its DNA. However, in conversations about the future of data and technology, it became obvious that a radical mindset shift was needed to enable the kind of transformation that was now required. Yet, even with such evident flows of natural creativity, it soon became evident that administering the medicine for addressing these ailments seemed far more painful than the challenges they were supposed to cure.

The initial hope was that the forward-thinking and creative team would be highly receptive to implementing urgent change. Yet I would soon discover an enormous gap between words of agreement and initiated action. As firm walls of resistance were swiftly put up by some, it became evident that while this highly talented and innovative group was open to adapting to changes within known paradigms – it struggled when it was confronted with a paradigm shift. Instead of being open and willing to experiment or test new ideas, key individuals within the group resisted the idea of a paradigmatic change.

It was easy to imagine how such a smart and talented group would be sceptical of such change. There was no shortage of skills, expertise and capabilities among the ranks of team members, who included experts in architecture and design approaches, such as Zachman, TOGAF and Kimball, which offered some of the most widely accepted industry standards. There seemed to be limitless backgrounds and expertise in a wide range of data and technology methodologies: including not only such modern approaches, like Kanban, DevOps and Agile, but also the more traditional Waterfall and Software Development Life Cycles (or SDLC).

Beyond expertise in traditional database technologies, such as Oracle and Microsoft's SQL Server, there was also an abundance of specific technology knowledge – including Search, NoSQL, Hadoop's Big Data Frameworks and Kafka. The firm had also invested in talent with exposure to all the major public cloud ecosystems, including Microsoft Azure, Amazon Web Services (AWS) and Google Cloud Platform (GCP). The labels and associated acronyms were endless.

What I found tough to swallow was that the group maintained a level of forbearance and collective curiosity that seemed a considerable contributing factor in previous successes – yet they somehow mustered a strong resistance to the paradigmatic transformation that now seemed so obviously required.

As I think back to the weeks and months of intense debate about how these painful challenges could be resolved and the fast approaching a cliff's edge averted, one thing was clear – most of the ideas came from me and a handful of others who, like me, had not enjoyed the extent of longevity that most of the others had within the Gaming Guru. Could this be coincidence or was there some relevance to the fact that most of these ideas were being proposed by those who may have been considered outsiders?

It was fair to admit that, at the time, my primary focus was not on the source of any ideas or solutions being proposed. My key focus was, instead, on the "to what end": on the challenges that we were faced with and on the ultimate outcomes we were determined to achieve. It is, however, also fair to admit that some of my ideas might have seemed difficult to stomach.

I recall being unafraid to challenge the status quo – going beyond being inquisitive about data and technology implementations to questioning the fundamental design principles upon which they were developed. It was like going beyond contemplating ways to resolve the issues with the fossil-fuelled engines – that have reliably ferried us from one point to another for many generations – to wondering if a radical transformation could mean that cars could actually be powered by alternative sources or that petrol and diesel engines could be eliminated altogether. It was perhaps like grappling with creative ways to address the awkwardness of the cables and wires that connected our household devices – in the past – to contemplating not having cable-free and wireless devices. In hindsight, it is clear that such first principles thinking seemed too novel and unorthodox for even some of the brightest people I have ever come across to contemplate.

Rishi, one of the organisation's most respected lead architects, was not shy about expressing his scepticism. "I really cannot see how such unorthodox approaches could deliver more superior results than the best of breed designs we have either already assembled or chosen to discard," he said. "And how can such novel ideas deliver tangible results in less than five years? In fact, we are almost definitely going to need results within five months."

"These suggestions align to no framework or pattern I have come across so far," another colleague said.

Yet another made an even more interesting comment. "In spite of a lot of this sounding like bending the rules, there is something far too common sense about this that makes me somewhat uneasy," he stated.

Tough as the results of such "first-principles" thinking were to swallow – perhaps even more so as the ideas being generated were considered not to have been entirely incubated from within – the group did maintain a level of forbearance and collective curiosity that seemed an undoubtable contributing factor in previous successes.

So, the big challenge was to secure the buy-in of the entire collective – as well as create enough confidence to enable the entire organisation to cross the chasm.

The world was a different place back then. Recent examples of adapting to new realities shaped by the Covid-19 crisis show just how much acceleration is actually achievable. In a recent conversation with a senior executive at one of the U.K.'s biggest retailers, I learned about a transformation that was previously deemed unthinkable. It was weeks into the first lockdown and not much in our day-to-day lives could have been described as "normal." What she told me gave me a sense of the immense scale of change happening in organisations across the globe: the retail organisation had not only brought its five-year digital transformation plan forward, but events of the day compelled it to fully implement the entire plan within five weeks.

And so, while the world was already changing rapidly in the years prior to Covid-19, the current scale and pace of transformation could not easily have been envisioned. In addition, paradigm-shifting innovations like big data, robotic process automation (RPA), drones, artificial intelligence, the cloud and the Internet of Things have been turbo-charging the move towards a world where business transformation possibilities make the desirable transition from endless rhetoric to limitless realities.

Why did the Gaming Guru's group of highly skilled and intelligent individuals seem – on the surface – to be so unreceptive to an opportunity for radical transformation? And why did an organisation so technologically advanced still find itself stuck and unable to answer questions like,

> How can we provide our customers with quicker answers? How can we better understand their underlying intentions to then meet them at the point of the greatest achievable impact? How can we get more value out of the data we collect? How can we keep our costs low while future-proofing our technology architecture and organisational design? How can we rapidly scale in markets that experience growth and manage our exposure in shrinking markets?

There had to be a better way. It seemed that the courage to *bend the rules* was required in order to achieve the necessary transformation but, in order to enable this, *old* rules had to be tested in *new* ways.

"We have to accept that we cannot expect new outcomes if we stick to the old rules," I told the team. "We need to become more comfortable with the discomfort of unlearning our old ways."

The new environment had to be enabled by a transitional architecture approach, underpinned by a decoupled and distributed data model. This would ensure that the system could be broken into tangible units that could be detached and replaced with minimal impact on the rest of the system. Most importantly, the system would need to be capable of seamlessly switching connectivity between old detached units and any new components engineered as their replacements as the underlying landscape evolved.

Yet, there were many complexities to consider for such an extensive transformation to be smooth and graceful – and components of the system needed to continue to function without interruption. As with the example of an aircraft, critical parts needed to be replaced without causing any disruption, and more importantly, without the passengers realising that essential reengineering was being undertaken mid-air.

Yet, how could we make such significant changes to a landscape with a supply chain that included hundreds of third-party integrations and with millions of customers from across the globe? How could we transform a digital system that was running 24/7 and had no significant downtimes through the year, a platform so transaction-heavy that it often processed more interactions than some of the world's most advanced stock exchange platforms? And how could we make such changes without causing noticeable disruptions to the organisation or its customers?

Some of the strategies for addressing these challenges came from the fundamental insights my eclectic background had afforded me. When I joined TAG, for example, I realised that before embarking on what would later become an audacious transformation, the situation required a comprehensive understanding. We undertook hundreds of hours of focused interactions like workshops and interviews, spanning revenue-generating verticals as well as horizontal areas providing functional support. There were also opportunities for one-to-one sessions and additional informal interactions.

The collection, consolidation and collation of comments captured through a series of workshops – which left no area across the entire organisation without a voice – revealed a number of insights, including the urgent desire to enhance integrity and trust.

The focus on trust that was apparent in finance workshops was no less palpable in sessions with teams working in compliance, fraud prevention or legal. Representatives from areas like marketing and pricing as well as revenue-generating verticals like personal direct, retail partnerships and commercial lines were also keen to point out that trust and integrity were critically important for their areas of responsibility.

So the question became: why did the data, AI and technology solutions currently being delivered to these functional areas not mirror the sort of alignment of vision that seemed so evident from the information gathered across the broader organisation?

Our insights would eventually enable us to gain significant alignment on our vision – as an essential requirement for moving forward.

Due to the similarities between this previous experience at TAG and the situation that we were now faced with at the Gaming Guru, I wanted to share some of the key insights I gained with Rishi in a one-to-one video call.

There were two underlying questions we had to address. The first one was, 'How do we simplify our data landscape in order to enhance operational speed and increase operational resilience?' Live system failures were rampant in those days, and the time it took to deliver data or analytic outcomes was frankly unacceptable to the business,

I said.

> The second question was, 'How can we be much quicker in our ability to satisfy requests for new services or changes to existing ones? And how can we ensure sufficient compatibility so the changes be achieved without disruption to our data pipelines, structures or products?'

I explained that our analysis revealed that one of the biggest challenges was that design efforts often started with data and jumped too quickly into technology solution mode – rather than starting with the right questions to help clarify the overarching challenge or purpose.

"This led to required outcomes that were challenging to deliver, enhance or change," I continued. "What was even worse was that the initiatives often delivered solutions that were suboptimal for the underlying challenges or opportunities that they were developed to address, since their problem statements had not been sufficiently understood to begin with."

In previous comments and questions, Rishi had made it clear that he was sceptical that the proposed unconventional approaches could deliver better results than the best-of-breed platforms the talented team at the Gaming Guru had either already assembled or chosen to discard. He struggled to see how something so novel could deliver tangible outcomes within an acceptable time frame.

I found that his questions, while demonstrating a healthy dose of creative curiosity, lacked sufficient focus on the overarching purpose of the required transformation – a situation not too dissimilar from what I'd seen in my early days at TAG.

Rather than approaching the discussion from the perspective of the constraints of the firm's legacy technology landscape, I suggested that a focus on the thoughts, approaches and strategies most likely to project the organisation's ambitions might be a better starting point.

Another common challenge I had encountered was a focus so narrow that it missed important information that might be found at the edges of pertinent use cases. In my experience, this often led to outcomes that didn't adequately reflect any inherent alignment present across organisational silos. Potential consequences included increased isolation of individual units and departments, which led to heightened *interactional friction* and the build-up of unintended obstacles.

My early exchanges at the Gaming Guru suggested that any solutions needed to be aligned with one central goal: achieving the most appropriate intersection between enhancing *interactional speed* related to the customer experience and continued growth enabled by *frictionless scale*. However, I knew that it could be just as damaging, especially for enabling robust data foundations for artificial intelligence, to pursue a focus so broad that it creates undesirable levels of inertia.

I was hoping to convince Rishi of the validity of our approach by sharing more information about our work at TAG.

> When we analysed a particular situation, where most of the foundational data infrastructure was sponsored by the finance department, we found that the subsequent design was constrained by the boundaries of their expectations – and was only sufficient for satisfying the required outcomes of key finance stakeholders,

I said, adding that such outcomes did not necessarily meet the needs of other teams or departments.

"For example, the strict filtering rules determined by finance led to situations where data sets, such as certain sales transactions, were filtered out of files and tables," I said. "This led to what I call the data black-hole phenomenon."

I explained how the *data black-hole phenomenon* was a pattern I found to be commonplace across the data value chains of a broad range of organisations and industry sectors – and how it seemed to be driven by the arbitrary injection of filters within data pipelines which progressively became challenging to detect.

This phenomenon first came to my attention in the early 2000s when I was leading Basel II regulatory data projects for large global financial institutions. In one such instance, I had uncovered a serious issue with a data warehouse that provided key inputs for critical counterparty exposure calculations. It turned out that a process – buried deep within the maze of data transformations responsible for delivering these key inputs – had some embedded exclusion logic, which effectively filtered disagreeable data into a specified data location for further processing. We would later discover that this location was not only undocumented but was also unmonitored, in effect becoming a black hole – and home to millions of dollars worth of missing data.

Years after this initial experience, happenstance presented me with yet another déjà vu moment when I encountered a data estate with similar challenges at TAG, which was at the time one of the world's most prestigious insurers. Particularly striking was the fact that the organisation's issues were not the result of a lack of investments, which is the commonly assumed culprit. Despite yearly budgets for data and artificial intelligence numbering well into eight figures, the issues had failed to be resolved. Numerous technology solutions had been acquired and tried, but so far, none had enabled effective resolution. The implementation of cutting-edge software – both in master data management and dynamic information warehousing – had been individually insufficient to address the challenge.

"That's interesting and clearly not so different from the kinds of situations we currently face here," Rishi admitted after a thoughtful pause.

"While the gaps created by this process were adequately managed to limit their impact on finance and use cases, like earnings, ageing and reserving, the implications for functions outside finance across the entire business were severe," I said.

The most obvious ramification was that data sets were either incomplete or unavailable to the broader organisation.

I went on to describe the consequences this situation had on both transparency and auditability – and ultimately integrity and trust. Senior professionals across the organisation commonly had to spend a disproportionate amount of their efforts on validating and verifying data outputs.

In addition, operational inconsistencies and data gaps – referred to as "destructive data changes" – also had implications for marketing and product teams, who needed to leverage data to gain insights related to sales attribution, promotion performance, customer analytics and more.

The reasons for such destructive data changes were numerous. They ranged from a design choice that discarded historical data and applied a current-state constraint on the data retained within data consolidation systems, to the approach to fixing data entry errors within operational systems. Yet, the inevitable outcome was unambiguous, including the challenges of keeping downstream systems synchronised with such frequent data changes, the difficulty with understanding the rationales that drive change or the trends to which they could be attributed, the implications on the operational speed of data flows throughout the firm and the increased challenge of traceability and explainability.

"Well, as you know, we have such challenges here too," Rishi replied.

"I do and this is why I find this previous experience relevant," I said.

To be honest, it would be no exaggeration to say that the impacts of such destructive data operations – on those teams working in pricing, fraud and compliance – were no less trivial than what you are experiencing here at the moment.

Over the next few minutes, I recounted how this challenge caused even more frustration when retrospective data updates rendered previously captured facts invalid, with significant implications for reconciliation, auditability and traceability across the firm. Operational overheads for such bulk updates were also huge and challenging to manage – with the impact on data platforms and technology teams uncomfortably severe.

"Well, that certainly resonates," Rishi said.

"The bulk updates required not only the management of significant workloads from a central data platform perspective," I said. "They also called for difficult-to-implement coordination across multiple downstream systems and consumers."

Rishi seemed particularly interested to learn that beyond coordination, some downstream systems also required data reloads and reprocessing – with consequences for both human and technology resources. He was also curious to know how we had gone about resolving these issues.

"Initially, it was quite challenging to gain sufficient buy-in to make tangible progress," I said. "However, by going back to the fundamentals – of each area's 'to what end' – we were able to rethink and simplify our design and approach."

I explained that by asking the right questions and applying *first principle thinking*, we had discovered that the finance department's imperative – to create data snapshots at will and reflect retrospective transactional alterations (which resulted in destructive data updates) – could indeed be achieved alongside the broader organisation's aim for transparent data integrity, enhanced flexibility and improved operational resilience.

"Remarkably, the design principles we evolved also had positive cost implications for both operational efficiencies and our ability to make changes without incurring systemic consequences," I said.

"I would certainly be keen to explore this further," Rishi replied.

I told him that we had leveraged the power of the cloud where appropriate, but rather than a "lift and shift" cloud migration, we opted for an in-depth exploration into how we could simplify our pipeline processes.

"It started with the realisation that data mutation in itself was not an underlying requirement for the finance department. In effect, data changes – such as updates and deletions – were not necessary," I said. "Instead, the desired outcome was to be able to summarise data for particular effective date ranges and to ensure that these summaries also represented the most accurate information available to the organisation at the point of asking."

We found that these data overriding processes were a design choice that seemed perfectly logical at the time they were made.

"Interesting," Rishi remarked. "Wasn't this the result of poor decision-making by the architecture and engineering teams and maybe an indication of their level of incompetence?"

"We found it important to set such judgements aside when we reviewed the data landscape," I stressed.

There were often good reasons for making what in retrospect seemed like bad design choices. In some cases, we uncovered challenging constraints, such as technology or human resource limitations either to do with skills or bandwidth. We've also seen situations where decisions made in the isolation of disconnected silos led to suboptimal outcomes in the larger context. There is also the possibility that each area's 'to what end' was not sufficiently explored and understood.

Ultimately, it was insights from our *first principle thinking* explorations that had provided the springboard for testing the hypothesis that data, once captured, did not need to be altered – and this led us to the principle of *immutability by design.* Much like one of the underlying key principles of a blockchain ledger, immutability implies that data would remain unchanged, unaltered and indelible. This enabled a key step towards satisfying the aligned "to what end" requirements of reconciliation, auditability and traceability for both finance and non-finance stakeholders. It was a powerful realisation: by enabling voices from across all the firm's silos, we had begun to find resolutions to entrenched – and previously considered unsolvable – challenges.

Another issue that needed to be addressed was ensuring consistency in outcomes. For example, an insurance policy was sold for $100 on day one, but when the customer was making changes on day two, he or she incurred a $20 administrative charge. This would imply a total income of $120 from this policy by day two – from both the original premium of $100 and the subsequent administrative fee of $20. While this might seem a straightforward situation to capture, the difference between the legacy implementation and the one demanded by the principle of *immutability by design* was anything but trivial.

For the legacy implementation, the effect would have been a destructive update to both the first and second event. A record of the combined income of $120 for the policy would be captured, yet this would be done at the expense of obscuring any evidence of the original – individually separate – $100 and $20 transactions. This created unintended consequences for traceability and auditability with associated implications for integrity and trust. It also led to gaps in delivering outcomes that could enable use cases from different areas across the entire organisation.

In contrast, the *immutability by design* principle would lead to the retention of both the original day one and the subsequent day two transactions, enabling on-demand aggregation to deliver the finance requirement while access to the details and the underlying evidence could enable accurate cross-departmental use cases.

However, some of the early concerns about this model involved scenarios where erroneous data entry had occurred. Stakeholders with both technical and non-technical backgrounds were asking, "Would that not require data to be legitimately overwritten?"

When I presented the example to Rishi, he was also curious about how this could be addressed.

"Interestingly, an answer to this conundrum came from the practices that the finance teams applied in such scenarios: the principle of the *application of movements*," I said. Rules that finance teams employ, as a standard, aim to deliver outcome consistency as well as perpetual transactional auditability. Among what are sometimes called the "golden rules of accounting" is the application of "debit movements," capturing positive financial entries like the individual $100 and $20 policy transactions, on the one hand.

"Credit movements," on the other hand, record funds that exit the firm, for example, when a retail customer would return a purchased item and receive a refund. In the insurance policy example, a similar effect would be realised if a customer made changes on day two that resulted in an insurance coverage that costs less. Such a situation would likely require processing a customer refund and applying a "credit movements." That's how the practice of the *application of movements* has the capacity to accommodate scenarios where changes to a policy lead to a reduction in the total payable premium.

I told Rishi that I had overseen the resolution of countless data incidents in the days prior to TAG's transformation, when our legacy approaches and processes were posing serious limitations. In one notable example, a customer service agent had added an extra zero to one entry.

"This ticket seems the most critical today," a service analyst had stated in a conference call. "A customer service agent seems to have erroneously keyed in $1,000 for a policy amendment that should have been $100."

At that time, the resolution involved authorising the reprocessing of all the transactions for the day on which the issue occurred, requiring a significant operational undertaking with numerous associated challenges.

"After our transformation, this sort of situation would only have required an authorisation for the entry of a credit movement to the tune of $900," I told Rishi.

At this point, he had heard enough to suggest that we bring some of these strategies to the broader stakeholder group.

I was happy to have gained an ally.

12

Beyond the Whiteboard

It was incredible to see almost all key technology stakeholders physically assembled in a single location. All the senior colleagues and technology partners from across the Gaming Guru's entire business – including product, marketing, finance, compliance and fraud – were present, along with notable stakeholders from a variety of technical domains, such as infrastructure, data science, architecture, engineering, project management and service operations.

The air was charged with anticipation – it seemed our preliminary individual conversations had created a mixture of excitement and anxiety. Bringing this group together felt like a major milestone but I knew that it was only a first step. We had to find a tone and topic that resonated across such different areas of responsibility and inspire ongoing engagement in our upcoming transformation journey. The start was promising since most participants were quickly making the switch from coffee chats to taking their places around the table, ready for the business of the day.

It had been weeks since Rishi and I agreed to get everyone together, yet it had taken excruciatingly long to get commitment for a group workshop.

"We just can't seem to align everyone's calendar," Rishi had said in the beginning.

While I didn't doubt this might be the case, I was convinced that more could be done to make things happen. Rishi suggested an executive mandate but I was not comfortable with the idea. A directive from the top would help to get everyone to the table but was unlikely to secure genuine and sustained buy-in. Instead, I was keen to engage with the individuals we needed to get on board.

DOI: 10.1201/9781003278276-16

There were some key influencers, and it sometimes felt like they determined the atmosphere: how receptive and open their colleagues were to discussing and exploring new ideas. These were the people I had to convince, and it had to be done face to face.

In addition to one-to-one meetings at my base location, the next couple of weeks saw me jump on planes to spend time at other sites. Although the approach seemed effective, the conversations did not go as originally expected.

Rather than a focus on what possibilities these new ideas could bring, concerns and fears of uncertain implications seemed to be front and centre in people's minds.

"So, let's assume this all works. Would we have the skills and know-how to pull this off?" I was asked in various guises.

I was clear about my expectation that skills and capabilities would not only need to evolve alongside the data technology landscape but also with the required shift in mindsets. I sensed that the underlying unease would be difficult to shift.

There were those who felt that some people would struggle to adapt and learn. Others assumed that some people would be left behind – through no fault of their own – and focused their concern on what might become of such individuals.

The conversations did not yield all the answers, but what they did deliver was a sense of "we are all in this together" and a renewed focus on the ultimate "to what end." They reinforced the reason why something radical had to be done – to address the pertinent challenges with the data and technology landscape and to ensure the organisation was viable in the long run.

"I have no idea what you said to the guys, but we seem to be making progress with diary alignment," Rishi said. "I suppose this could also be a coincidence."

When the event was set and attendance confirmed, it felt like a major accomplishment, but I knew we were just getting started – and the battle of hearts and minds was far from won. The session of the day started with a recap of where we were as an organisation.

"If radical change is not achieved within a matter of months, we are toast," a senior executive had emphatically told me in confidence. The audience in the room seemed to share this level of urgency – and the sense that we were speedily approaching a metaphorical cliff's edge with our data and platforms.

I raised the fundamental questions we were looking to resolve: "How do we simplify our data landscape in order to enhance operational speed and increase operational resilience?" And,

> How can we be much quicker in our ability to satisfy requests for new services or even changes to existing ones, and how could such changes be achieved in such a way that we can ensure sufficient backward compatibility to avoid unwelcome disruption to our data pipelines, structures or product lines?

"Although one of these problem statements is clearly focused on the operational side of things and the other is focused on delivery, both are unmistakably centred around speed," one participant remarked.

"Absolutely," I said. "In fact, within the larger framework, I have specific points that are referred to as the *speed injection model*, which we could touch on later if time permits. But first, let's take a look at the broader piece."

I went through some of the discussion points I had covered in preliminary calls with Rishi, including *the principle of immutability by design* approach.

As I explained the principle of the *application of movements*, and how it provided capacity to accommodate the capture of multiple events and enabled a win-win scenario across disparate organisational silos, there was concern about potential inconsistencies that could be caused by backdated effectiveness: a relatively commonplace situation where an event occurs in the past but we are only made aware of its occurrence in the present.

"What if a customer moves house but only informs us months later. Would that not require both the customer's address plus the date this change was effective to be updated or changed?" a senior marketing stakeholder asked. She was particularly concerned about the implications for marketing consent, especially as General Data Protection Regulation (GDPR) was ushering in new and increasingly stringent regulations regarding the protection of personal data privacy across the European Union. Based on a set of seven core principles and mandating eight far-reaching rights for individuals – including "the right to rectification" of personal data and "the right to erasure" which is often referred to as "the right to be forgotten" – the regulation places stringent requirements on firms to ensure that the core principles are applied and that any individual rights related issues are responded to, addressed or resolved within stipulated timelines.

The marketing stakeholder's concern was hinged on the fact that, if the Gaming Guru's systems moved to prioritise the capture of the point in time that an event occurred – or its effective data – over the point at which the firm became aware of the event, "we could find ourselves in a very awkward position when looking to either monitor or demonstrate our compliance," they suggested. This was a very valid concern. For instance, in the case of the moving house analogy, the system timestamp capturing the point at which the customer actually moved house – as opposed to the point at which the information was received – would have put us on the back foot from day one.

Such concerns served as a reminder that the new approach needed to deliver better outcomes across the board – and address the challenges we faced with the legacy retrospective data change regime. I explained a simplifying technique for keeping the point of an event's occurrence (such as when a customer moved house) separate from the point at which the organisation becomes aware of it (such as when the customer informed us of the change in circumstance).

Called *the principle of timestamp separation*, the intentional separation of effective and knowledge dates – and their associated timestamps – further underpinned *the principle of immutability by design* approach as well as created a level of robustness and sophistication not previously available for data exploitation and integrated analytics.

Beyond enabling basic data analysis, it helped to facilitate sophisticated time-series use cases, and this provided an essential advancement for our data science and artificial intelligence capabilities.

From a customer relationship management perspective, it could lead to fine-grain identification and analysis of trends in such illusive measures as tastes and preferences. For data modelling, combining the principles of *timestamp separation, immutability by design* and the *application of movements* would allow for significantly more flexible and adaptive designs, including the implementation of slowly changing dimensional structures.

More broadly, *the principle of timestamp separation* combines well with other principles to provide adequate support for the application of the "observe, learn and automate" pillars via real-time analytics. This enables crucial machine-learning-powered "signal from noise" use cases, which can help to identify the best buy and sell opportunities for financial products like equities, predict the time to maintain critical machines before they experience failure, or adjust prices based on customer profiles, behaviours, risk assessments, value predictions and so on.

"Some of these principles just seem common sense," said a participant from the far end of the room. "So, if there are no major catches, then why are they not used more widely?"

"I often wondered about that myself," I responded. "While I have seen some of the principles applied separately, in all my experience and industry exposure, I've very rarely seen them come together like this."

It was indeed strange that these simple principles with such powerful effects were not more widely applied. From my experience, I deduced that one reason could be that people get used to how things have traditionally been done and sometimes fail to take a step back far enough to challenge the reasons for doing things a certain way.

For example, some design principles had been developed in the days when data storage had been exorbitantly expensive and when data redundancy was a key driver for the architecture of data or technology platforms. Even though circumstances have changed, most of the design principles driven by such historical constraints rarely get revisited or fundamentally reviewed. Similar outcomes are the result of a need to create physical indexing structures and the need to predefine referential keys and master them as structural constraints within data platforms. With the emergence of modern data platforms, a number of such rigidity advancing and flexibility limiting technology constraints are increasingly becoming concerns of the past. Yet, countless conversations across multiple organisations and across numerous industry sectors made it clear that such advancements were not as sufficiently exposed to professionals as a radical departure from legacy design concepts clearly demands.

"We also have to remember that not all firms are focused on solving the organisational silo dilemma or looking to address challenges with *interactional friction,*" I said, explaining that not every organisation was compelled to prioritise enhancing *interactional speed* and continued rapid growth enabling *frictionless scale.*

At this point, I noticed a significant level of engagement across the room, which helped to set the stage for the extensive material we had to cover. We next discussed how the *immutability by design* approach led to *the principle of natural granularity.* Its implications were that every event, every interaction and every transaction was individually captured and immutable – with every raw data capture kept materially identical to the truth at its point of capture. It may not have been a specific objective for most of the stakeholders, but this shift presented some positive unintended consequences. Perhaps the most significant was the impact that natural granularity had on bringing various disparate functions of the organisation together.

Unsurprisingly, the data scientists, statisticians and data analysts in the room were most notably excited about the prospect of having access to sets of data that were potentially much closer to the raw and original state than the data to which they had become accustomed.

"It's a dream come true," an excited data analyst declared.

> Having access to all this raw data at their natural level of granularity significantly simplifies my analysis. It means I don't need to generate fake data, develop arbitrary apportionments or play any number of the tricks I previously had to employ due to the gaps that data aggregation or just missing data caused to my analysis.

However, benefits went far beyond the volume of data available for insights, statistical analysis or machine learning model building.

One significant advantage could be seen in the area of data validation and testing, and I had observed this impact when I was working with Albert, the data science leader at TAG. As one of the world's largest insurance companies, the firm had sunk eight-figure budgets into data and technology year after year. Yet, for a long time, Albert's team had habitually spent disproportionate amounts of time on verifying data sources. They also spent much time and effort in manufacturing controlled data sets as a means of getting around the challenge of sporadic data updates and data mutation. These efforts were further compounded by the requirement for additional storage and resources that the situation compelled.

All this changed with the presence of natural granularity – and the associated absence of data mutation, which meant that controlling source data sets to enable credible model training and model validation were significantly less challenging. It was also fascinating to see how these benefits spread into functions like finance and compliance. With data no longer being overwritten, reconciliation moved away from being an uncomfortable art to being a predictable science.

Technology personnel also heaved a sigh of relief as they experienced a significant drop in the costs and efforts historically drained by ad hoc data movements or reloads. There were also sizable reductions in the demands for unplanned infrastructure provisioning, which had positive implications on the IT budget and also reduced the amount of friction associated with integrating incongruent technology components.

This new alignment also brought various functional areas together. It felt like the situation had evolved to a level of convergence that cut across the entire organisation as if a common language had emerged to enable frictionless communication.

Data was traceable and auditable. The *principle of natural granularity* also increased the ease of explainability and data audits, which were essential requirements not only for governance and compliance teams but across most silos of the firm. And the finance department had renewed confidence in the reconciliation of the numbers produced and insights delivered by analysts.

When a compliance manager said, "I feel like I could take half the day off and still get all my work done," this didn't sound as far-fetched as it would have only a few months prior.

Among the most common criticisms of this principle were its preservation of higher volumes, its requirement for intelligent design skills, and – as is often the case with high-value advancements such as artificial intelligence – its need for more compute resources. Another concern was that the principle discouraged pre-summarisation of data. Any required pre-summarisations had to be conducted separately to ensure that they were non-destructive and were only acceptable by exception.

Yet the substantial benefits seemed to outweigh these concerns. In addition to anticipated outcomes, unintended consequences included the connection of previously incompatible silos from across the company and reduced frictions previously associated with both individual and cross-functional interactions.

In our meeting at the Gaming Guru, the morning session was spilling over into the lunch break. The thirty-five minutes following the presentation felt like an interrogation, against the backdrop of the four key *operations-focused* design principles projected on the whiteboard:

- *the principle of immutability by design*
- *the principle of the application of movements*
- *the principle of timestamp separation*
- *the principle of natural granularity*

Questions were flying in, thick and fast. Not all of them were easy to answer.

"This does not follow any known pattern. How can we be certain it will actually address our challenges?"

"It seems so far from anything we've ever done. Even if this could work, how can we be sure we can get the right skills to implement it?"

"How long would it take to rethink everything we've ever built, or is that not what this would require?"

"Is this not going to be much too costly to achieve?"

"How can we shorten the time it would take to deliver tangible value through these approaches?"

"How can we ensure that new things built in this new way do not break old things built in the way we currently build our data pipelines?"

These were just some of the many points raised for discussion before lunch.

I explained that in order to achieve the radical transformation envisioned – and to do so gracefully – the new environment had to be enabled by a transitional architecture with a federated data model at its core.

"Aside from the *operations-focused* design principles already discussed, there are a number of helpful *delivery-focused* design principles that I have come to rely on to enable the kind of transitional architecture we would need," I said. "Such design principles would ensure backward compatibility, data pipeline adaptability and the iterative delivery of tangible value into production."

I clarified that the principles we had considered so far were primarily focused on the first key challenge: how to simplify our data landscape in order to enhance operational speed and increase operational resilience.

The second half of the session would predominantly focus on *delivery* and look to address the questions: how can we be much quicker in our ability to satisfy requests for new services or changes to existing ones? And how can these changes be achieved in a way where we can ensure sufficient backward compatibility to avoid unwelcome disruption to our data pipelines, structures or products?

I recounted a recent conversation with a key stakeholder that illustrated why this change was so important.

"I asked her why she seemed so hostile towards agile, and her answer was quite blunt," I told the room.

> She did not really care about agile, but instead wanted to get much more tangible value over much shorter spaces of time. However, it was clear that this was not a selfish desire from an impatient stakeholder. In fact, it was a reflection of the emerging customer landscape.

Over the years, we've seen customers getting more and more demanding. While this behaviour is often attributed to generations X, Y and Z, there is increasing evidence that these changes are happening across the board, although to varying degrees.

Everyone seems to want a much quicker and more personalised service than most firms across sectors have ever delivered. We also see the effect of customers being more digitally inclined, which was already noticeable before the coronavirus pandemic. With customers increasingly hooked on their phones, tablets and other mobile devices, this has meant that organisations have to look to artificial intelligence and similar emergent paradigms to meet this new demand for evolving and delivering products and services.

In the retail sector, firms are desperate to take out the frictions and barriers that hamper true multi-channel customer interactions. The benefits on the consumer end are huge: a relationship with a service provider that is truly seamless; where transitions between physical and digital do not have a degrading effect on experience; and where we can get what we want without the pains and traumas of long delays.

In the financial sector, there are significant benefits for those who are able to address the ineffectiveness of agent-to-client pairings. For example, wealth managers – even those with no shortage of killer products and star sales performers – often struggle to get the optimum pairing between their agents and client prospects, even when signals clearly point to the availability of money in motion.

In the insurance sector, for instance, companies are seeking opportunities for moving away from the traditional model, where customers are just "bill payers" with whom they typically interact about once a year, either at policy purchase or renewal time – towards a partnership-type and value-based relationship.

These radical shifts across the sectors are evident across numerous developments. Real-time data, telematic devices or mobile phone apps, for example, can allow for more flexible and accurate motor vehicle insurance pricing, with tangible outcomes like "pay-by-mile" and predictive, flexible risks-based insurance coverage. Insurers are also increasingly offering customers incentives like "safe driving discounts" to reduce accident risks, limit large losses and decrease fatalities.

Yet, in a future world, customers want even more. Imagine a situation where claims could be automatically issued, perhaps based on real-time data from a home appliance or a car. Imagine the assessment of claims being done instantaneously, either via a mobile phone camera or a drone. Imagine insurance claims being settled swiftly rather than customers having to make endless calls.

Beyond these scenarios, imagine a world where the most distressing accidents and losses could be avoided altogether – through the combined effects of the predictive power of artificial intelligence and the effective outcomes driven by intelligent interventions.

Rather than discuss the benefits of agile or of any technological advancements, these were the kinds of possibilities that stakeholders were keen to discuss. Yet, achieving such a world required a different approach to the one that had become commonplace across firms of all kinds.

While the cloud, software as a service (SaaS) and a host of solution providers have inundated the marketplace with a wide variety of transformational tools and services, the approaches and methodologies for implementing data transformations appear to have been left behind. Many questions have been asked about why such a significant gap between tools and methodologies has emerged.

One possible answer considers the speed at which the current industrial revolution is evolving.

Towards the end of the 18th century, radical technological advancements made mechanised industries the backbone of the societal economy and ushered in the first industrial revolution. Driven by the important invention of the steam engine, this period was characterised by substantial increases in coal extraction. Powering steam engines and more, coal was central to the new energy system. Railroads were built out and the entire economy accelerated.

It would be another century before significant technological changes drove the emergence of three new sources of energy: electricity, gas and oil. They powered the development of chemical synthesis and steel, turbocharged industries and also enabled the creation of methods of communication, such as the telegraph and the telephone.

The paradigm shifts that underpinned the second industrial revolution around the end of the 19th century also empowered the injection of more speed into our economies and daily lives – by enabling the inventions of both the automobile and the aeroplane.

Yet another century later, towards the end of the 20th century, the world would witness the emergence of another significant force: nuclear energy. This industrial revolution brought forth the rise of electronics, telecommunications and computers. From then on and into the early 21st century, these advancements drove further innovations, including in space exploration, biotechnology and industrial robot automation.

The fourth industrial revolution – often referred to as Industry 4.0 – has, however, caused some controversy. Firstly, in spite of broad acceptance, including from credible organisations such as the World Economic Forum, there is – as yet – no absolute consensus about its existence. Some people insist that the next revolution has not yet commenced. Those who accept that it is underway, on the other hand, point to the seismic changes that are already evident in our daily lives but warn that its full magnitude is yet to be understood.

Secondly, proponents also suggest that rather than a linear trajectory like previous revolutions, today's pace of change is exponential. They believe that a fusion of technologies has led to a blurring of the lines of separation between the physical, digital and biological spheres.

Some controversy is also driven by the fact that there wasn't a century-wide gap before its onset, as was the case with previous revolutions. Instead, the current revolution started at the dawn of the third millennium with the one thing we now use every single day: the internet. It has powered the development of such technological tools like the internet of things, blockchain, big data, the cloud and artificial intelligence, injecting even more speed into our existence. This industrial revolution seems to *bend the rules* we have become accustomed to, including our standard measures for radical innovation cycles.

One school of thought suggests that the shortfall of human methodologies related to technological tools is due to the shorter time span between the third and the fourth industrial revolutions – which amounts to half the time of the previous cycles: on the average being a century between one revolution and another. It is understandably argued that humans have struggled to adapt to this faster-than-usual pace of change, with insufficient time to gain new skills and inadequate opportunities to embrace new ways of working. Regardless of whether the term "revolution" is applied to the current radical technological advancements, their impacts are impossible to deny and their speed of evolution impossible to ignore.

At the session with Rishi and the other delegates at the Gaming Guru's internal conference and after a compressed lunch break, it was obvious that the big question was, "How do we bridge the widening gap between technological tools and human methodologies?"

There have been suggestions that the answer lay in bringing about a mindset shift. What was required was an openness to new ways of thinking, working and interacting.

Yet another common thread cut across every one of our industrial revolutions so far: the growing need for the *injection of speed*.

I remembered an incident not too long ago, while I was consulting at the Media King. A C-level executive had endured a severe dressing down from the CEO, which set off a cascading ritual.

I ran into the executive when our coffee rounds coincided. After giving me a generous helping of the bitter medicine he had just endured, he added,

> Do you know the trouble with data departments like ours? The trouble is, we get data flying in at such speeds and from a variety of sources. We know this speed is gaining momentum all the time, with the increase in the use of digital channels and the increasingly demanding customers, who want it all now. And what do we do? We slow it all down, with our tediously slow processes, our spaghetti ETL and our complex byzantine data warehouses or data lakes.

On the surface, this might have come across as castigating but the underlying message was clear: our data landscapes had unintentionally become riddled with steps that slowed the pace as well as erected hurdles or even brick-wall-like barriers to both data flows and data products engineering.

However, what followed was a period of radical candour at the Media King that delivered insights about the structures and processes we had long taken for granted. One of these discoveries concerned constraints that came from our continual race towards database integrity perfection. As a result, data was often stuck partway through our pipelines. For instance, if a service was sold before its master data had been propagated through the data warehouse, then all subsequent sales transactions would be stuck. Or, if a customer moved to an address yet to be updated on the post office's database, then it was often challenging to push the customer data into the appropriate tables and data sets.

Another insight highlighted designs that unnecessarily forced dependency management. One scenario illustrating this was when data about a customer's complaint arrived at a time when some of the customer's details were blocked, for example, due to new address details not matching our master data. This data was then stuck in a holding pattern and did not provide the kind of early visibility opportunity desired.

As with most areas of life, perfection in data quality was impossible to achieve and challenging scenarios were hard to avoid. What's more, our efforts to prevent them had slowed the pipeline down, causing a delay to the resolution of such issues or even leading to complete data blockages in some cases.

It was also eye-opening to discover the intrinsic challenges that came from a tight coupling of data structures – and the processes by which their content was transformed any time an adjustment was necessary. This presented a nightmare for managing change, even when it was not driven by demand for new data or analytics products. Especially disruptive were the effects of changes to source systems.

"We are clearly in a bit of a mess," one colleague declared, stating the obvious. "The business is forecasting astronomical growth while our landscape struggles to cope with today's demands."

After a number of fairly impassioned debates, another team member demanded, "So, rather than sit here agonising about our collective hindsight, should we not channel our brain power towards getting ourselves out of this mess?"

During the strategy session at the Gaming Guru, Rishi and other colleagues were keen to hear my recollections of the strategies that had helped to fix such gaps.

"I have found that keeping focus on organisational ambitions has always been essential, whether you are looking to solve organisational silo dilemmas or address challenges with *interactional friction*," I said, reiterating that much of the presentation of the day had so far centred on sharing principles that were predominantly focused on *operations*.

For *delivery focused* principles, on the other hand, I had found it useful to pay particular attention to enhancing both testing and deployment flexibility.

"When we think along these lines, strategies like continuous integration and continuous deployment become absolutely essential," I explained.

It is very helpful to be able to use adaptations of techniques like blue-green deployment and feature-toggling to flexibly drop and extract code from production environments with minimal impacts on status quo operations and customer experience.

> However, I have also seen that these strategies – even when they are employed for data and artificial intelligence – were, by themselves, insufficient for addressing the impacts when we were dealing with the kinds of hurdles we uncovered at the Media King.

I went on to explain how we evolved a number of principles, predominantly focused on delivery, to tackle these issues. I recounted how we used what

I sometimes refer to as *biological data links* to address the challenges resulting from enforced data constraints, which were akin to implementing slowly changing dimensions via the conjunction of immutable natural keys with naturally immutable event timestamps. These were available as a result of the combination of *the principle of timestamp separation* with *the principle of immutability by design* – and helped to reduce the complexity of dependency management and latency in the data pipeline. The approach also enabled more flexible data loading, more focused testing and considerably more code deployment flexibility.

The use of *biological data links* also allowed us more flexibility in our ability to reformat, restructure or remodel data without wide systemic impacts across the landscape.

To enable a seamless transformation, including one towards the cloud, it is additionally essential to establish a transition-friendly hybrid architecture. This is particularly important since "big bang" transformations are not only inherently risky but also unlikely to deliver tangible benefits within acceptable time frames. They often end up being altogether unviable.

I explained how, by using an approach I have sometimes called *smoke and mirrors* (though with a positive twist away from its traditional connotations), we were able to deliver logical abstraction – additionally increasing the flexibility and adaptability of underlying physical data structures. This was sometimes achieved using any combination of layers of service APIs, customised views and creative metadata.

I also shared how we ensured backward compatibility by never destroying defined data structures, an approach that also established a practice where data columns or data fields were never removed, though data attributes could always be appended. This principle helped to reduce complexities of change – as well as diminished potential downstream implications for adjustments that were made further up a data pipeline. Its introduction also increased code deployment flexibility and meant that more focused testing could be applied to intentionally isolated changes.

By employing *the principle of backward compatibility* by default, we wanted to ensure that new things did not have adverse impacts on old things.

One of the more controversial approaches I had found useful related to silos – and I called it *the principle of intentional silos*. Much like the methodology used for the design and architecture of microservices, this approach was focused on breaking big things into smaller units. At its core, it was an important enabler for delivering new data products or services – or for applying changes to old ones – at pace. It also allowed the required level of separation for an individual product or service to be designed, developed, managed and scaled independently of all others.

Combining these principles helped to create a new paradigm where continuous integration and continuous delivery enabled the kind of flexibility that approaches like feature toggling and blue-green deployments allow. What's more, alongside this flexibility, we saw some unintended consequences that included enhanced *interactional speed* and support for *frictionless scale*.

Another example, again from my work at TAG, can help to illustrate the power of these principles. At the beginning of my engagement there, I had been summoned to the office of one of the most senior executives in the entire group. She expressed extreme frustration about the state of data across the firm and told me that she had been waiting over five years for the organisation's data to yield tangible results to satisfy some of her most critical requirements. She had also been concerned about the operational performance of some existing data and analytics products, including one that sometimes took over three weeks to deliver tangible insights.

The application of *the principle of intentional silos* was instrumental for the development of a cloud-enabled data factory and the radical transformation of the entire data pipeline. It allowed us to make some of our most critical legacy processes not only up to thirty times faster but also many, many times more resilient, in spite of some of these legacy processes being underpinned by antiquated technologies that were much beyond their sell-by dates.

As a direct consequence of the seismic shifts that this principle empowered, some of our most critical processes, which had in the past taken over three weeks to deliver outcomes, were now capable of producing such results within three hours.

A less obvious benefit of *the principle of intentional silos* was the empowerment of teams – and enabling them to be sufficiently autonomous. This was an essential ingredient for our transformation from a legacy, location-centric culture into being virtual by default. While our transformation started well before the global coronavirus pandemic, the transition towards a virtual culture provided an important foundation not only for today's ways of interacting but also for a distinctively different post-pandemic world.

It is also a beneficial approach for creating clear lines of sight between an individual product or service and its value proposition – and can support the monitoring or visualisation of such effects in real-time. This enhanced visibility was particularly helpful for TAG since it simplified accountability and reduced the complexity of conversations about funding or budgeting.

In data science and analytics, the *principle of intentional silos* creates opportunities for intentional separation of entities across the entire value chain: from feature selection and engineering, to signal generation and detection – and even beyond the prediction of outcomes – to intelligent interventions.

"So, four helpful *delivery focused* design principles that we can add to our toolkit are: *the principle of intentional silos, the principle of biological data links, the principle of backward compatibility,* and *the principle of smoke and mirrors,*" I said as time crept towards the end of the Gaming Guru group workshop.

I also explained that some of these approaches are best used in conjunction with the *operations focused* design principles already discussed.

And while these principles were broadly technology agnostic, there were certain technological scenarios that substantially increased their effectiveness.

"A move to or towards the cloud was one of those clear accelerators," I said. adding that the opportunity to provision and scale technologies in the cloud could deliver significant additional benefits. "However, I have to stress that when it comes to the cloud, simply lifting and shifting the legacy data pipelines or target data structures is only going to offer limited short-term advantages at best."

The most effective solutions require rethinking "how" we build resilient and scalable data platforms and data services. Yet, these would all come to nothing if they did not drive us towards our ultimate "to what end." Our ambition? To deliver both sustained growth and stability as well as empower the achievement of the central goal: finding the most appropriate intersection between customer experience enhancing *interactional speed* and continued rapid growth enabling *frictionless scale.*

As we walked out of the room after the session, which had started with scepticism and gradually progressed towards productive consensus, I heard someone from behind call my name. A colleague hurried to catch up with me.

"So, be honest with me," she said.

From where did all the insights leading up to these *first eight principles* actually originate? Did they come from some textbooks, your university education, or some training courses? I know they were obviously honed through the analogies and experiences that you shared, but there must have been some foundation, no?

"I appreciate the curiosity," I said. "But in all honesty, I have yet to come across any textbooks or training material that articulates these approaches. Perhaps we could work together to go beyond the whiteboard and actually bring it all together?"

13

Leaving People Behind

A few days after the highly successful conference, the euphoria started to wear off. We knew there were credible ways out of our data and technology challenges at the Gaming Guru but felt a certain apprehension about our ability to bring it all together. In a video call with Rishi and a few others, concerns that had been concealed for a while suddenly began to be exposed.

Our colleague Ladi, along with two or three team members, was adamant that a package of strategies put together by the senior technology executive leadership team would do the trick. Others were less convinced. An impasse on the approach for moving things forward seemed inevitable.

With consensus out of reach, we postponed a decision on the roadmap for change to a subsequent meeting and focused our immediate attention on measures where an agreement could be achieved. These included securing resources, setting up environments and establishing a sustained period of experimentation. However, there was no doubt that we had to get the organisation on side, that we had to win hearts and minds for this to have a chance of being successful in practice.

Ladi – along with those who similarly had confidence in a top-down package of measures being rolled out by the senior technology executive committee – would later find that a less orthodox approach would be our eventual path for addressing cultural challenges and for enabling the success of the architectural experiments we were conducting and which were subsequently embraced across the entire organisation.

"The principles you suggested all make logical sense and actually seem simple. But it is clearly a paradigm shift from where we are right now, and that still makes me feel quite nervous, to be entirely honest," Rishi said near the end of the very productive call.

DOI: 10.1201/9781003278276-17

In spite of his evident unease, I was pleased to see that Rishi was increasingly open to owning this. His support and leadership were vital since he was one of the most respected architects at the firm. I suspected that his concerns about a status quo – where operational performance was rapidly spiralling downward in a world where speed was becoming the currency of success – outweighed his discomfort about how this paradigm shift might work in reality.

Kriszta, a highly regarded senior architect who knew the entire landscape better than most, openly voiced her concerns about the disharmonious interactions between the individuals considered to be fortunate enough to work at the organisational headquarters and those who belonged within the sizable network of teams spread across locations outside the head offices.

"You are right to be concerned about that, Kriszta," I said. "I actually think that this could be one of our biggest challenges – more so than the technology shift in itself.

"I understand how the proposed changes can make people nervous, but there are ways we can mitigate that and hopefully deliver these benefits safely," I continued. "I think it is key to not only focus on all the benefits that this should bring but also capture the full range of concerns we might have as a group."

After a brief pause of consideration, Rishi responded,

> That's an excellent idea. It is so interesting to think that whenever we propose solutions, we typically put significantly more emphasis on selling the benefits, especially for the solutions towards which we might be favourably biased. The approach you are suggesting would effectively ensure that we design with both strengths as well as potential weaknesses front and centre.

"Absolutely. That's a very good way to make certain we don't get blindsided by our enthusiasm," I said, explaining that the most credible way to address such concerns was to embark on a number of safe and controlled experiments.

"It is difficult to find reasons to disagree with this approach," said Kriszta.

> And I agree that crafting a set of safe and controlled experiments is a credible next step. But my big concerns are how broader buy-in is going to be achieved and how we could ensure that – as this transformation progresses – people do not get left behind.

These were valid concerns, yet the temptation was to brush them aside with such banal platitudes as, "It will all be fine. There is nothing to worry about."

However, this would not have been ultimately helpful or sustainable, so I instead shared a story about an experience where such fears did come to pass and needed to be addressed.

A few years before, as I was working with EIG, I was in a scheduled call with a senior executive that had been booked to discuss a data analytics transformation that had been ongoing for a number of years.

The transformation had been plagued with numerous setbacks, with most stakeholders, at first, blaming silos among teams and across underlying data repositories. It was clear that the firm's embrace of *delivery-focused* design principles had enabled significant progress: the use of *biological data links* was already helping to simplify the challenges resulting from enforced data constraints as well as reducing some of the complexities of dependency management across the data landscape.

There was also evidence that the application of *the principle of smoke and mirrors* – and the logical abstraction it facilitates – was enabling additional flexibility and adaptability for the underlying physical data structure.

In addition, the use of *the principle of intentional silos* was starting to bear fruit. The purposeful separation it facilitated was enabling individual data products and services to be designed and developed in parallel. And the resulting clear lines of sight between individual products and their distinctive value proposition were simplifying accountability and reducing complexities typically associated with funding and budget-related conversations.

Teams were also becoming more empowered due to *the principle of intentional silos*. There were signs that teams embraced new ways of working and were progressively able to act autonomously – a clear difference from how things had been before.

Yet, despite these advancements, I knew senior executives at EIG wanted more.

Preparing for a memorable Zoom meeting, I wondered what aspects of the transformation the senior executive might want to focus on.

"Look, I must first and foremost thank you for the efforts thus far in what is turning out to be a tangible transformation," said Susan, a polite, courteous and warm senior executive. "We are seeing more progress than I ever remember seeing throughout my years here – and I have been here a while. However, I must confess that I have some concerns."

I was surprised when she described her concerns, which were not primarily related to our approach nor the speed of change.

"People have been coming to me because they are worried that the technology is changing too quickly," she explained. "Everything around them is changing rapidly and they are worried that they may not be able to adapt quickly enough."

Susan made it clear that she was as concerned about her people as she was about other impacts of our current data, artificial intelligence and technology transformation journey.

"We have been here before multiple times, and some of these memories remain raw in our minds," she said, recounting the story of a previous attempt of implementing organisation-wide technology changes. They involved migrating technology platforms from an AS400-based application stack to one built on Oracle database technologies and powered by Linux infrastructure.

"It was quite a change," Susan said. "From a business operations perspective, it was a move away from green text on black screens – where navigation was based on memorised keyboard keystrokes – to a world of mouse clicks or drags and drops."

The situation led to the establishment of two camps: the legacy camp and the strategic camp, which went beyond technology teams. There was soon ample evidence of a kind of "discontinuation resistance" across multiple organisational silos.

Team members in call centres and in other operational support functions were attached to the legacy ways of working and the tools to which they had become accustomed. In technology teams, the battle lines seemed even deeper.

Among the strategic camp, the opinion circulated that the "fat cat" members of the legacy camp were only resistant because their "ludicrous" contractor and consultancy fees were at risk of evaporating overnight. One contractor seemed to epitomise the image of the "overpaid consultant," Susan said, describing him as a "fairly arrogant chap" who was always fashionably dressed in designer labels and drenched in expensive aftershave as he drove around in his fancy red sports convertible.

She recalled a period of endless bitter "us against them" battles which, at some point, became so contentious that there had even been suggestions of sabotage.

"The atmosphere was absolutely toxic," Susan said. "Things got so bad that we had to reverse a big migration drive and were so close to a decision to abort the project altogether."

"So, was the thinking that the negative impacts of silos between teams was to blame for these historical challenges," I asked.

She confirmed that *interactional frictions* between teams did indeed play a part, but a thorough review after an eventually successful technology rollout showed there was more to the story.

"The findings were eye-opening," she said. The report had discovered that the "discontinuation resistance," which had at times escalated into a full-scale confrontation, had in fact masked much deeper *concealed concerns.*

> It turned out that rather than a battle of envy over an arrogant chap in designer labels and a fancy red sports convertible, the real issue was a fear that lots of people had of not being able to sufficiently adapt to this new world,

she stated. "So, the fights were apparently not much more than just distractions. People were just afraid of being left behind."

That's when "the penny dropped" for the senior executive team. While they had managed to pull off a reasonably successful technology transformation, there was no path in place for a people transformation. In retrospect, it seemed plausible that this lack of consideration was, at least, partly to blame for the drawn-out battle between the two camps.

Susan's big concern was that – much like in the previous battle of the legacy camp versus the strategic camp – many people would get left behind – yet again – even as our data, artificial intelligence and technology transformation were set to succeed.

Not only was this different from what I was expecting to hear, I also found it refreshing that a senior executive was so concerned about the fate of her people. What's more, the situation she described was not unique – I have seen many similar examples throughout my experience. Interestingly, I had seen no differences between the age or size of a firm or even industry sectors: transformations seemed to habitually pitch old against new and people against technology. I have seen countless individuals and teams experience such painful scenarios. No doubt, some people are dealing with similar challenges even now. And such distressing circumstances are concerning for those who've gone through them before as well as those encountering them for the first time.

"You are absolutely right to be concerned," I told Susan.

> I've seen it numerous times. An organisation announces a technology transformation – and there is a genuine sense of optimism in the air – but

reality unravels through time, this happens. Unfortunately, these fears are not unfounded in many of these situations. In effect, when the dust settles after the transformation, it is not only the old or heritage technologies that get left behind – it's the people.

For many years, I wondered, "Why do we continue to see this happening? And what can we do to reduce these negative impacts, not only on our people but also on our organisations?"

It was sobering to consider the ramification of such situations: the anxieties and battle lines, the disruptions and counter-productive increase in *interactional frictions*.

Yet, my experiences also suggest that the challenges underpinning these causes are by no means insurmountable. I wanted to share some of these previous learnings with Susan.

"One of the reasons this happens is that in a lot of these cases, project delivery is prioritised over people development," I said. "While such prioritisation might present some short-term benefits – such as a higher speed to market and a lower cost of project delivery – they often come with significant challenges."

Among such challenges were operational ownership, cost of maintenance and a firm's ability to make future changes, I explained. "And these are over and above the human cost: the impact on morale, the effects on well-being and other associated implications."

Another example, and perhaps a most extreme situation, came from my recent work at a public sector agency, where I had come in to help ensure the delivery of a sensitive project that was under the scrutiny of both legislative houses. In the framework, through which the project was supposed to be securely delivered, there were elements that seemed very constructive and others that appeared less likely to lead to productive outcomes.

The overall project was broken into a number of core work streams, each contracted to be delivered by a third-party technology integrator.

On the one hand, this was a very creative approach with numerous benefits that included reducing the risks associated with only having a single supplier as well as ensuring competitive pricing and incentivising high-quality deliverables. On the other hand, this created an atmosphere of seething distrust between individual suppliers with competing agendas. The tensions beneath the surface seemed ready to boil over at the slightest of provocations. The resultant environment, even when it was superficially calm and without incident, seemed to do little to reduce *interactional frictions* between the independently run project-delivery silos.

One of the ways of mitigating the effect of these silos was through the project's formidable oversight and governance structure. The project management office created for this purpose was overseen by another third-party firm that was not associated with any of the other workstream suppliers. Representation from the public sector agency's internal resource capability was broadly absent.

This was another double-edged sword. The separation of concerns and the allocation of accountabilities to different third-party companies created a sophisticated system of checks and balances that prevented potential turf wars. Yet, it also led to highly unfavourable conditions for cultivating internal ownership and sustainable accountability. There also seemed to be one additional flaw that some considered a glaring oversight by the overarching architects of this project's framework.

"All these external companies seem unified by a single common objective: longevity," Jodi, an internal senior manager, once told me over lunch. She suggested that regardless of which part of the projects they were responsible for, they all sought creative ways to increase the durations of their engagement and the size of their account.

One obvious challenge with this framework was the lack of internal and permanent staff involvement across project delivery streams.

Of the work streams, which throughout my engagement numbered between seven and eleven, there was not a single one that had more than two permanently employed staff. By my recollection, work streams typically had just one internal representative, and it was not uncommon for some unlucky work streams to end up with none at all.

There was little doubt that the extensive use of such sophisticated frameworks for the engagement and onboarding of third-party consultancies and systems integrators provide a lot of adaptability and scaling capability. Much like the cloud enables technology transformations, sophisticated frameworks for the engagement and onboarding of third parties allow organisations, such as the public sector agency, to rapidly ramp up the supply of resources to meet demand as well as flexibly scale these resources down when downward fluctuations occur. Such flexibility is extremely challenging to deliver with the formal routes for securing or reducing internal resources.

On the flip side, the knowledge gaps that such approaches create – between those who develop new products or services and those with whom operational accountability should lie – can inadvertently exacerbate the *interactional frictions* that are often blamed on organisational silos. Too many of the people who ultimately assume responsibility for the products or services, which have been developed by external third-party resources, have lamented about the ills of "black-box deliverables" that eventually "just get chucked over the fence."

In one instance, a substantial black-box product was deployed into an operational environment, having been built utilising technologies that were completely alien to the people who were tasked with its day-to-day management and potential maintenance.

Another challenge stemming from approaches that favour outsourcing and that Jodi was particularly concerned about, was the high levels of anxiety and uncertainty that typically accompany these strategies. Beyond the often less tangible lowering of morale, reduced cooperation and even increased apathy that such situations fuel, I have seen incidences of increased stress levels, depression and other significant mental health challenges over the years.

In a particularly memorable one-to-one conversation, a colleague told me,

> I cannot help but feel that I am being left behind. Our legacy technologies are insidiously being replaced right under our noses, yet internally, we don't have the necessary skills or even the time to develop these new skills. If I'm honest, I am becoming more and more convinced that this is all part of a grand plan to not only replace technology but replace our teams as well. It really does feel like a kick in the teeth after all the hard work we have put in and the commitment that we have shown over the years.

He made it clear that he was "fed up and progressively unmotivated," and that this sentiment was shared by other individuals on the team.

I thought of relating this experience to Susan in our call about the Gaming Guru's transformation, but since we only had a few minutes left, I chose to instead focus on a win-win scenario at TAG that might be adaptable to the situation at hand.

At one point, our ratio at TAG had been 80 to 20 in favour of externally sourced staff, not only leading to disproportionately high outflows of jobs from within the internal walls of the firm to the confines of various third-party suppliers but perhaps more worryingly leading to significant bleeding of knowledge and capability through the outer skin of the organisation.

"It was an extremely challenging situation," I told Susan.

Aside from a lopsided resource pool, which posed significant challenges for internal knowledge and strategic capability building, there were a number of policies that were ineffective when it came to addressing challenges – our central project resource allocation policies among them.

"Our core policy was quite simple. It started with looking at the top priority projects on our universal portfolios and was followed by an assessment of the projects' skills requirements," I said. "People from our entire pool, which included both internal and external resources, were then allocated to individual projects based on a skills match. This ensured flexibility for the delivery of projects and for the managers accountable for their execution."

However, while this allowed project c somewhat erratic ebb and flow of resource demand and supply – it also came with detrimental implications.

"From an internal employees' viewpoint, this approach was anything but favourable, since the skills assessment and matching mechanisms made no distinction between internal and external staff," I said. "The sole focus was on competencies and capabilities."

This led to some project teams being unbalanced, with some having only 10 per cent internal representation and some not having any internal representation at all.

"In these cases, the knowledge required to effectively own and operate the project's deliverables were at risk of walking out the door when the contracts with the external consultants expired," I recounted.

As a result, internal staff felt intense anxiety on such consultant handover days. "Rumour had it that some staff intentionally took sick days off to avoid being involved in such 'over the fence' handover sessions in order to reduce the chance of being earmarked to own such deliverables," I said.

Another big challenge this situation presented came from the fact that projects were typically insular, with little or no interactions between project or operational teams. Some saw this as one of the most damaging manifestations of the silo dilemma.

Another – and perhaps the most detrimental – consequence was that projects were often prioritised over people.

"Since our legacy approach seemed to prioritise projects over people, this made it difficult for internal staff to make and advance any career development plans," I said. "Aside from the more obvious implications, such as poor capability building, motivation and morale, one of the eventual consequences of this deficiency was its negative effect on staff turnover."

This is bad news, especially as one of the key determinants for staying competitive in today's world – especially in the field of data – is talent.

In the recent past, competitive advantages could typically be gained via capital. Since technology was expensive – and required extensive upfront investment to amass sufficient resources or capacity to enable viability – this favoured established organisations and presented barriers for start-ups. Sustainability challenges for established organisations were often related to indeterminable time-to-value appropriation as well as poor – and potentially financially catastrophic – decision-making.

Yet, in today's world, barriers to entry are diminished by one of the most outstanding technological innovations of our time: the cloud. With the cloud, access to abundant managed resources is easier to obtain and available on a "pay as you go" and "only pay for what you use" basis, completely wiping out antecedent technological advantages of large and established traditional organisations.

This has driven a considerable adjustment in the balance of power, giving rise to garage tech companies growing into giants at speeds previously unthinkable – and leading to the demise of established icons that have struggled to reinvent. It has also moved the battle lines – for competitive advantage – from technology and capital to people and talent.

The wars fought along these new battle lines have led to unprecedented wage inflation across data and artificial intelligence related professions, as well as affected other areas. In what is increasingly a candidate-led market, organisations are now compelled to make innumerable adjustments – to working conditions, culture and even technology choices – in order to attract the best talents and persuade them to stay.

At TAG, this shifting environment posed an additional challenge to the already problematic 80-to-20 external-to-internal staff ratio.

"We knew that project requirements were very important, and it was in no one's interest to cause avoidable disruption to their delivery," I said.

> But it was also clear that the status quo was unsustainable and trending towards a total erosion of internal knowledge capability. Frankly, the only viable option was to create a shift that would result in a win-win situation that was acceptable to all.

A key element of this new approach was a gradual *ratio rebalancing* of teams. The main thrust was to acquire sufficient critical mass of internal talent for distribution across work streams.

Another important element of the proposal was the establishment of academy-style guilds of specialist practices – for the purpose of the novel development of new team members as well as the continuous improvements of established internal capabilities.

An interesting twist to the implementation of the academy was a method sometimes referred to as 80/20 reversal, which was based on an essential principle for capacity planning. Its premise was that for the continuous improvements of already established internal capabilities, 20 per cent of an individual's bandwidth would be allocated to skills training and development, while 80 per cent would remain as available capacity for advancing a projects' deliverables. For the newest and least capable team members, the numbers were reversed: 80 per cent of an individual's bandwidth would initially be allocated towards skills training and development, while 20 per cent would be available for working on projects.

To enable the success of both the continuous improvements and novel development strategies, we knew we needed to go beyond skills training and ensure that a more sustained level of capability development was achieved. An approach, which is sometimes referred to as *purposeful placements*, was envisioned to get people working on the projects that were most closely aligned with the individuals' skill sets they were in the process of developing.

Another important element of this strategy was a focus on enhancing existing third-party relationships. In spite of our situation of skewed team ratios and a short supply of internal resources, we were determined to stem the tide of critical organisational knowledge "walking out the door" as contracted external consultants came to the end of their engagements and their resources were suddenly unavailable to us. It was obvious that these operational risks were far too costly and that creative alternative interventions were urgently needed. As a means of mitigating this threat, the new approach proposed a *blended by default* strategy for all project teams, which enabled the reduction – or even the eradication – of third-party single points of dependency across all projects' deliverables.

"As we moved to make these changes, one of the first things we had to do was to dig deep into the sources of 'discontinuation resistance' we saw from a number of project managers," I said.

As we started the transformation, the initial days were marked with intense scepticism from many key players – some out in the open and some behind closed doors. As with the majority of the projects I have encountered, most of these reservations seemed to – yet again – be underpinned by *concealed concerns*.

Although there seemed to be reasonably broad acceptance of the *blended by default* strategy, all other proposed changes initially faced considerable opposition. There were fears about a perceived loss of bandwidth, especially with the proposed *80/20 reversal* strategy for the *novel development* of new team members. There were also concerns about a potential dilution of expertise due to the *ratio rebalancing* strategy, which required bringing in new team members who required time to get up to speed. Other comments exposed fears about a perceived reduction in flexibility, particularly as the *purposeful placement* strategy proposed movements of internal resources that were a radical departure from the current approach to resource allocation.

In order to move things towards a desirable outcome, we had to transform the vagaries of intangible benefits and concerns into palpable risks and value propositions. Our approach was to develop a cost, time and knowledge retention capability model to allow for the visualisation of the most optimal ratios – and to ensure points of diminishing returns were pre-emptively highlighted.

This enabled objective debates and resulted in a favourable win-win situation accommodating both projects and staff – finding the most appropriate intersections between the desire to ramp up at pace and the need for continued sustainability.

Looking back, the strategies we applied to achieve successful outcomes seem simple. However, in matters that had connotations for the well-being of team members, there were two fundamental matters that had to additionally be resolved. The first was getting beyond what seemed to be a complex cocktail of undecipherable agendas and the *concealed concerns* that lay buried beneath. The second was striking at the heart of the *value proposition* that needed to be brought to the surface.

Susan listened attentively as I shared insights from these experiences.

"Thanks, Ed," she said at the end of our call. "I am quite pleased we decided to record this conversation. I am looking forward to following up with a broader session."

14

To What End?

One Thursday afternoon, I picked up my phone to find an unexpected LinkedIn message from a senior global credit risk executive.

> *Hi Ed,*
>
> *Great to see you becoming ever more influential in the world of data science, leadership, etc. I wondered if you'd be able to spare me some time for a call to allow me to pick your brain towards developing a roadmap for my organisation? Very much at the beginning of the journey with a lot of ideas but never enough time or capability!*
>
> *Thanks,*
> *Nancy*

I was surprised as well as intrigued. We had barely been in contact for years after working closely together at an organisation considered one of the U.K.'s "Big Four" clearing banks and one of its largest retail banking providers.

I responded by saying I was happy to offer as much support as I could, and we soon had a phone call arranged.

In our call, Nancy explained that she was looking for trusted guidance on how she could move her firm from "manual to automated." She was keen to hear my thoughts on how the use of analytics, machine learning and other data science approaches could help to accelerate this ambition.

The business had been largely client-focused in the past, providing facilities to the lower end of the market. However, some large capital injections over the past few years had boosted its ability to attract great

DOI: 10.1201/9781003278276-18

minds and lure star players away from the competition. Yet, this feat hadn't led to the kind of progress Nancy had anticipated.

> It sometimes feels like I'm just having lots and lots of conversations with people who want to provide guidance and advice on how to build a tech strategy or a product strategy or on what kind of enablers we need from a data perspective,

she said. "There is what seems like constant and endless talk about the myths around AI. And an endless stream of very clever PhD consultants have been coming in, but none are able to solve our problems in any tangible way."

This was the conundrum she wanted to discuss. "I would love to get your perspective on this, because I know how important sound foundations and expertise are."

I assured Nancy that such situations were not uncommon. I had dealt with similar challenges many times, sometimes being called to review situations after multiple rounds of external input had failed to deliver desirable outcomes.

"I was often told, 'We've had these consultants for five years, but they haven't built anything,'" I said to Nancy, adding that at this point, many firms had already spent seven or even eight-figure sums.

"It is even more difficult when so much has already been committed, not just in financial terms but also in damage to trust and integrity," I said.

I had found that the higher the investment that had been sunk into such projects, the more challenging it seemed for firms to cut their losses, even when it was clear that the chances of success were slim.

My mention of "trust" triggered a response from Nancy.

"I absolutely agree," she said.

> Across the executive team, we find that these situations are impacting our ability to build trusting relationships. When I reflect on past years, it is clear that we have become less and less trusting, and this makes it more difficult to get into new vendor or partner relationships.

I had observed this recurring theme many times and knew it had the unintended consequence of increasing rather than reducing *interactional frictions* – the opposite of what organisations were keen to achieve.

Yet, I also knew that a lack of trust was a particularly challenging situation to address.

In today's world, the economic importance of trust cannot be overstated – it goes well beyond its established "soft" value. Numerous sources, including analysis by *Our World in Data*, show a "very strong positive relationship" between a nation's wealth and trust. This resurgent emphasis on the economic value of trust has also brought the question of "who can we trust with our data?" into sharper focus. Media attention has recently highlighted data breaches, such as the high-profile Cambridge Analytica scandal, where data inappropriately harvested from up to 87 million Facebook profiles was used to provide analytical assistance to the 2016 presidential campaign that saw Donald Trump emerge as the U.S. president.

However, it is clear that data vulnerabilities expand far beyond Facebook likes and Twitter tweets.

Our data offers insights into who we are, where we live, work and travel, how much money we have and what we own, and about the people and issues we care about.

Some people have wondered why risks of data breaches seem to be increasing rapidly in recent times.

"Haven't we always had data that defines us in this way," is a question I often hear. While that is indeed the case, I believe there is something fundamentally different about the data landscapes that are currently emerging.

Our personal data has never been as easily accessible as it is now. In the distant past, such data would have been stored in diaries, letters, address books, filing cabinets or other similarly secure locations. More recently, our data would have been sheltered in our home computers or our company's human resource applications.

In today's world, however, the mobile phones, tablets and apps we use to simplify aspects of our lives have made such data more easily accessible.

Yet the implications of this emerging data age go even further. Data on things that may previously not have been openly expressed – such as our thoughts, intentions, emotions, beliefs, likes and fears – can now be captured and processed at ever faster rates.

The creation, capture, collection and conversion of these new data assets form the foundation of a new data economy. Now, the value of a customer-facing organisation no longer solely depends on the products and services it offers today but on its ability to continuously improve consumer experience to retain loyalty for the future.

Respected commentators including Rachel Botsman have openly explored the importance of trust for emerging economic systems. In her TED Talk on collaborative consumption and reputation capital, she discusses how the data that enables the creative connection between you and I on platforms like Uber, Google, Netflix, Amazon, Tik Tok, Instagram, WhatsApp, Zoom, Airbnb or Tesla is inadvertently creating a trust-driven economy – one that will see the emergence of a globally dispersed trust-based currency.

While organisations have always faced trust-based issues, there has been a notable shift from a sole focus on hard facts, such as the accuracy of financial numbers, for example, to softer reputational concerns like credibility, influence and status.

Research already suggests that firms typically lose over 5 per cent of their market value within the first five days of a single trust-damaging data leak or hack, which is likely to be only the tip of the iceberg.

The world's cryptocurrencies, some of which have recently seen heavy institutional backing by the likes of Tesla's Elon Musk, are underpinned by decentralised blockchain-powered "trust" networks, in effect creating "tokens of trust" that can be exchanged for financial value. Since both international regulators and global financial leaders are convinced that the timely availability of trusted data is not only "a key step but an important step" for mitigating the risk of global financial systemic failure, the link between trust and data cannot be overemphasised.

As my conversation with Nancy progressed, I found that the trust issues she was concerned about were not limited to external third-party relationships.

"The challenge is not only with engaging vendors," she said.

> It is somewhat embarrassing to admit that we sometimes struggle internally as well. There is not a huge level of trust shared between the senior leadership and our tech teams. I think the trouble is that fingers have just been burnt far too many times.

While this was obviously uncomfortable for Nancy, I assured her that it was not uncommon. I also wondered if this erosion of internal trust had partly driven the firm's decisions favouring external engagement. In addition, I couldn't help but notice an even broader implication: the increasingly important correlation between trust and value.

Nancy's comments seemed to suggest that when less tangible value had been received over time – both internally and externally – trust had diminished.

When I pointed this out, she concurred.

"That's interesting," I said. "perhaps even more so because I have, sometimes, found the reverse to be the case."

I described an example of a damaged vendor relationship I had previously inherited.

> At the time I took over, the relationship was so poor that it had gone from a significant growth account and a partnership that was meant to help implement our transformation to one that no one wanted to be associated with,

I said.

I then explained how we achieved an unlikely turnaround of this relationship and that this experience made me realise that an *alignment of incentives* was key for establishing or re-establishing trust.

"As we progressed through crisis talks with the vendor, it became clear that the incentives that sat between the vendor and our organisation were far from being aligned," I said, "The vendor had assumed that the engagement was focused on delivery and had built a model to fit that perceived objective while the organization was instead keen to prioritise ongoing capability building."

The vendor's approach – of creating a "black box" team with minimal interaction with internal teams and with all the knowledge necessary for the maintenance or operations of the delivered solution buried deep in internal structures – was also far from helpful. This led to the perception that our organisation was going to end up with yet another unsupportable delivery, similar to past negative experiences with projects contracted out to third-party firms.

> As soon as I realised that a lack of *alignment of incentives* was at the heart of the matter, I set out to clarify that our key priority was indeed capability building, especially since the solutions that were being developed required new technologies and new skills,

I said.

This realisation led to a significant shift in the resources the third-party vendor was going to make available to us. We also resolved that the "black box" approach had to be changed to a more open and blended approach, where projects included individuals from both internal and external teams – and with firm commitments for unhindered bidirectional information flows.

We arrived at a win-win situation that not only radically reduced internal tensions but also formed the basis of a cooperative relationship that helped to diminish *interactional frictions*. Benefits extended beyond our organisation. As a consequence of this reinvigorated relationship, the overall contract size remained materially unchanged and one of the vendor's executives told me in confidence that margins remained just as healthy.

It amazed me that achieving an *alignment of incentives* was not a standard prerequisite for entering engagements or was perhaps one that was not sufficiently focused on. However, there seems to be a global trend in favour of such an approach. One high-profile example left the world baffled about how a country of less than half of the population of New York found itself spearheading one of the world's fastest vaccination drives: the deal that saw Israel beat out much bigger countries and territories, such as the United States and the European Union, in the race against Covid-19.

In spite of a global shortage of Covid-19 vaccines, Israel secured a steady stream of vials and inoculated a larger share of its citizens than any other nation by striking a creative deal to lock in early supplies of the Pfizer-BioNTech vaccine.

While disruptions to global supply chains caused delays for the procurements of vaccines in other countries, the supplies coming to Israel's Ben Gurion Airport remained plentiful and uninterrupted due to a unique "vaccines for data" deal.

In the Real-world Epidemiological Evidence Collaboration Agreement, the nation of less than 9 million citizens promised Pfizer a vaccination campaign at an unprecedented rollout speed. In exchange for a supply volume enabling a vaccination rate ten times quicker than the United States, data from the country's centralised collection of medical statistics promised the pharmaceutical giant an opportunity to study "whether herd immunity is achieved after reaching a certain percentage of vaccination coverage" for any distinct territorial body or contiguous populations.

Entitled "Funding/Contribution of the Parties," one key section served to confirm that "no funding" was to be provided under the agreement and that each party was to fund its individual commitment under the agreement – whether that was for the timely and accurate collection of data or the efficient and secure exchange of it and any resultant analysis. This is an example of the kind of cooperative deal that is perhaps more widespread in textbooks than in real-life scenarios – creating a successful win-win situation based on clear *alignment of incentives* for both parties.

In my exchange with Nancy, she was interested in exploring ways to "start afresh" due to the realisation that the organisation had to rebuild its data, tech and digital strategies from scratch.

"We are a multibillion dollar company, yet we know we are so far behind where we could and absolutely should be," she said. "And, I must admit that, this is very frustrating."

Nancy revealed that the executive team was not overly concerned about the here and now, since the firm was still financially buoyant. The impressive performance numbers and even more remarkable projections she shared illustrated the source of that confidence.

"But we are very well aware that complacency could be our Achilles heel," she said.

> So, I'm thinking that what we need now is to bring together a small and focused group of experts, who have earned their stripes, who have the breadth of knowledge and experience and who could probably help us craft a strategy for what we need to do now to ensure we can stay abreast of – if not surpass – our competitors.

"Look, Nancy, I can help with that," I said.

> From my network, I could get a small group assembled before long, but isn't there a risk that you just end up in a similar place, with 'endless streams of very clever PhD consultants', just like you spoke about earlier?

While I agreed that talent was key to getting the organisation where it needed to go, I was not convinced that this was the best place to start.

"From listening to your personal experience, which resonates with much of what I have seen in my work and heard from others, I would consider both talent and technology to be solutions," I said. "However, rather than start with a solution, I would recommend starting with the problem – which would be a much stronger place to start your journey from.

> For me, it needs to start with *vision*, and I don't mean this only from the viewpoint of grand organisational visions that capture airtime at town halls and are printed on T-shirts or mugs. I am talking – more specifically – about the smaller visions that underpin such grand visions: the tangible use cases and ideas the organisation is looking to achieve and the small things that need to happen to bring these big ambitions to fruition,

I continued. "But it doesn't stop there. For such an approach to be truly effective, these visions must reflect the organisation's value propositions."

I explained that I considered this powerful combination of "vision and value" the aggregation of a firm's "to what end."

To illustrate why I find it vital to start there, I described the example of a recent project. I was working with a world-class retail company with both in-store and online presences at a time when Covid-19 response measures triggered an economic downturn. The company's 30-day free return policy for most purchases comes at a huge expense, including such liabilities as shipping and restocking costs, damages and merchandise carrying cost, store associate time and non-congruent inventory as well as store transfer costs.

"The firm's ask was simple: build us an artificial intelligence solution that can predict the return of an item even before it is actually purchased," I said. "And this made sense, especially since the intention was to offer such customers a 10 per cent discount to reduce the incidence of returns."

While this seemed a logical intervention – after a well-performing predictive model had been built in the final stages of the project – it suddenly became apparent that something was not quite right.

I asked for data on the current cost of returns since I was keen to put this figure alongside the aggregate cost of paying out a 10 per cent discount for every item that the AI model predicted would be returned. However, I learned that this value was unavailable – neither the historical average cost nor the overall cost of returns seemed to have been previously analysed. Although this exposed a vital flaw, the situation was not without reason: such calculations are very complex and have to be considered at item level. However, the information gap led to more questions than answers.

"How was the value associated with the effective delivery of this AI model to be established?" I wondered. As a further complication, the fact that natural occurrence of items that are returned is far outweighed by those that are not – presenting an imbalanced classification problem – there were also challenges with determining the optimal model accuracy parameters that would deliver the most appropriate outcomes.

In the absence of easy answers, I felt compelled to look for the closest possible estimation. The resulting cost of return approximation – alongside a triangulation of a set of targeted intervention strategies (such as final discount offers linked to no return), a set of assumptions (such as a customer's propensity to accept a final discount offer) and a range of AI model outcomes – enabled us to present a predictive range of returns on investment.

To our amazement, this proactive exercise revealed that the cumulative net effect of an intervention lacking in individual context sensitivity – such as the original blanket 10 per cent discount the retailer had proposed – could actually lead to millions of dollars in negative investment returns and financial losses as well as other unintended or potentially damaging consequences.

I related this example to Nancy to illustrate the importance of starting with vision and value, but there was one more essential element to the approach that I wanted to share.

"It is also essential to consider the obstacles that prevent the realisation of such visions and the value they should bring," I said. "It is an equally important and essential piece of the puzzle that I sometimes refer to as VoV, for *vision, obstacle, value.*"

We briefly talked about what some of these obstacles could look like.

"I recently ran a data strategy review for a large gaming and entertainment business which had enjoyed sizable growth over the past few years," I said. "However, the leadership team was acutely aware of the risks of complacency that such past successes could bring."

In one memorable meeting, the company's executives shared some specific concerns.

"Forty-nine per cent of our market is under eighteen, so below the age of eligibility for most of our products," one said, expressing her worries about the risks of sudden and radical shifts in customer demographics. Yet alongside such concerns, there was also an abundance of ambitions and vision. As one executive said, "Given our data, we could become the Google or the Facebook of the gaming industry."

There was nothing flippant or frivolous about these visions, as they were backed by significantly substantiated value propositions.

If our projections were anything to go by and we are also able to get to where we want to be with our data, we could be looking at a 40 to 50 per cent uplift on each of these products within a twelve-months window, and that's without raising operational expense spending,

one management executive told me.

Another suggested,

Since the small-scale experiment we conducted a couple of months ago yielded 13 percent growth in just two weeks, we are confident that applying significant scale can bring massive rewards. And we would have no hesitation in committing the necessary level of investments to make this happen.

This prompted the questions: "What was stopping these visions from being realized? What obstacles stood in their way?"

It was fascinating to hear the answers pouring in.

"I think it's a lack of leadership, from a data point of view," said one.

"It's accountability and leadership," said another. "It's certainly not a lack of investment capital. The money is there, so our obstacles have more to do with ability."

The technology teams were no less frustrated.

"Most of the time, we are unable to anticipate the changes, and that's not only system changes but also business growth and associated data complexities," one senior technologist complained.

"I would say our biggest challenges are at least partly to do with the complexity and inflexibility of our systems," said another.

While the list of challenges seemed endless, the overarching sentiment was that resource capability and organisational frictions were the biggest obstacles to gaining significant benefits from data.

On the one hand, it was clear that the firm was well structured, with vertically organised and location-centric units underpinned by a large and mature agency network. On the other hand, both opportunities and challenges – related to data – cut horizontally across the entire structure of its vertical silos.

It was clear that the technology landscape should be refreshed. Yet, there was also consensus that changes were not likely to deliver sizable benefits without an underpinning strategy to address the *interactional frictions* that existed between the organisation's verticals and its horizontals.

All this resonated with Nancy. "I came to you with a challenge but now realise that I might have been somewhat constrained in how I was contemplating resolving it: it now clearly seems like we were too quick to jump to people and technology," she said.

She pressed me for more on my VoV approach and asked if I could support her firm with trying it out. I agreed to contemplate how best I could offer some assistance to help drive their transformation, and she thanked me for my advice before hanging up.

A few weeks after this engaging conversation, I received an email from Sarah, a colleague I had worked closely with at BBG. It came out of the blue since we had not been in touch since our intensive collaboration on the heels of the last economic crisis.

Sarah had come across an article I had recently posted on LinkedIn and suggested we catch up.

In her usual fashion, Sarah started our conversation with a bombshell, as she gleefully announced her new senior role at a niche data insights and commercial advisory organisation with expertise in helping financial technology firms attract large clients and their investments.

Sarah was keen to hear my thoughts about the market implications of some emerging trends concerning digital, data and technology developments.

I was equally keen to gain some insider intelligence on how things shaped up after my engagement with BBG ended, and especially how the contentious data disclosure conundrum was internally resolved.

"Resolved?" Sarah laughed. "I won't quite call it that, to be honest. Yes, we did make some good progress but when I moved on a few months ago, things were still quite a long way away from utopia."

I observed that Sarah hadn't changed much at all. She still wore her heart on her sleeve – openly showing her emotions rather than keeping them hidden.

Over the course of our conversation, she shared what progress had been made and what challenges had remained unresolved. She told me about situations that were even more dramatic than the crossfires I had witnessed at BBG – tales about unresolved silos, about deeply entrenched and diametrically opposed camps, about dogged standoffs and unhelpfully divergence, and about continuing conundrums and never-ending paradoxes.

Yet, she also recounted moments when change appeared possible, when unhealthy competition shifted towards cooperation, when relationships edged away from trust deficits towards trust equity and when a clear path to resolution seemed to be exposed and within reach.

"There were those who remained deeply entrenched in individual camps that harboured diametrically opposite ideologies that seemed to exist at the extreme ends of the spectrum," she said.

Yet one thing was obvious: to resolve the silo conundrum – and to confront the paradoxes that lay at the heart of the disclosure dilemma – we had to dig beneath our hidden biases and go to the core of what we were actually trying to achieve.

There were moments when we were able to shift our focus away from our differences, away from our firmly held views on what was right or wrong, away from divergent positions on under-disclosure versus over-disclosure, away from perceptions of the ills or benefits of silos – and instead direct our energies towards our 'to what end' and our ultimate purpose,

Sarah continued. "In these moments, I saw glimpses of opportunities for tangible progress, for the kinds of possibilities you so often talked about, Ed."

> I saw potential for the *frictionless interactions* that you thought possible and that we so desperately needed. It sometimes felt like we could get there if we could get more people focusing on our ultimate goals – and holding firm to the practical and tangible rather than hypothetical or the theoretical, if more people were unafraid to set aside old things and willing to receive and internalise new things, even if that sometimes meant bending the rules until the rules had caught up with such new trends,

she said.

> It felt empowering to see that the potential was there, if only we could persuade more people to feel bold enough to question the way things have always been done and try safe experiments. While there were moments when this dream seemed within reach, it was also clear that there was a hell of a lot more work to be done.

I found it fascinating how my interactions with Sarah so long ago had triggered a significant transformation in her outlook, which had become more closely aligned with the most effective approaches for bringing it all together.

While our paths had diverged, her experiences had led her to conclusions that were very similar to my own insights: that making data work is seldom only a matter of applying new-age approaches, like Agile or DevOps, and is not only about embracing the ready-made solutions that continue to emerge from the cutting-edge tools and techniques that the cloud, the Internet of Things, blockchain or artificial intelligence bring, and is most certainly not only about investing in the obvious trio of platforms, people and processes.

Yet, like too many of the executives and professionals I encounter in my day-to-day interactions, Sarah had conspicuously missed a most fundamental of truths: that making data work additionally requires the sort of creative talent and leadership that is equipped to determine the most appropriate combinations amongst the multidimensional array of complexities which are essential for the skillful pursuit of every individually unique "to what end." Only by doing so would we be able to truly accelerate through the most effective path towards bringing together the most appropriate intersections between a win for one and a win for all.

Appendix

Some Key Terms Explained

TO WHAT END

For most of us, the question "to what end?" serves to connect us with an underlying goal or purpose. However, I have found that explorations of this question are seldom as straightforward as they seem and that the understanding of such fundamental objectives often requires in-depth assessments of potential results and thoughtful analyses of the possible implications of interventions. In addition, outcomes can be significantly improved when there is clarity and cross-organisational alignment on the ultimate "to what end."

CONCEALED CONCERNS

Concerns typically arise when we are faced with situations that cause anxiety or worry, and organisational change and transformation can present such challenges as they force us to learn new skills or adapt to new realities. Yet I have found that openly expressed concerns are often only the tip of the iceberg, with the bulk of discomforts hidden beneath the surface. Concerns may be concealed due to fears of exposing insecurities and vulnerabilities or, alternatively, because we fail to recognise their origins. For any work in organisational transformation, a deeper understanding of where underlying apprehensions come from, and what causes them, is essential.

INTERACTIONAL FRICTION/FRICTIONLESS SCALE

Interactional friction is encountered when points of contact, obstacles or other constraints slow down organisational processes or hinder the flow of information. Such blockages, which can come from barriers between people, systems components or both, can be caused by a variety of factors, including organisational silos, suboptimal technology integration, system architecture challenges, excessive bureaucracy and the human environment. As a result, friction can hamper growth and cause disruptions to efforts to increase the scale of delivering products and services. Frictionless scale refers to the reduction or eradication of obstacles to organisational adaptability or the advancement of a firm's ambitions.

SYNAPTIC CONNECTIVITY

A Stanford University study found that while our neurons – the brain cells primarily responsible for storage, processing and transportation of information – have sufficient capacity to make our brains the most advanced information repository in the world, it is the synapses – the bridges that facilitate the connections between these neurons – that enable a 25-fold increase in its sophistication. In effect, it is these synaptic connections that give our human brains the adaptability, capacity and scale that set us apart across the natural world.

CONNECTING SILOS

Silos are controversial. On the one hand, they are criticised for causing disjointedness, fragmentation, inconsistency, poor standardisation, missed opportunities, poor accessibility and duplication. Some critics even consider silos to limit knowledge sharing, innovation and value consolidation. On the other hand, supporters of silos hail their ability to simplify interdependencies and value assessment, increase resilience, resource separation and focus, enhance visibility, prioritisation, autonomy and flexibility. Connecting silos is the creative approach for combining all of the advantages with strategies to ensure that any potential suboptimal implication is avoided or significantly limited.

FIRST PRINCIPLE THINKING

Over a thousand years ago, the renowned philosopher Aristotle defined a first principle as "the first basis from which a thing is known." Utilised by many great thinkers, it has most recently been popularised by Elon Musk, who consistently applies the approach to his unending conveyor belt of radical innovations. At its core, first principle thinking is about breaking a process down to the fundamental parts that are known to be true – and building up from there. It is an approach to problem-solving that requires digging deeper, discarding any unfounded assumptions until we are left with only fundamental truths.

IMMUTABILITY BY DESIGN, THE PRINCIPLE OF

Much like one of the underlying key principles of a blockchain ledger, immutability implies that data would remain unchanged, unaltered and indelible. Immutability by design is an approach to building data landscapes that embrace this principle and employ it in designing data structures and their associated data flow pipelines.

THE APPLICATION OF MOVEMENTS, THE PRINCIPLE OF

Bearing similarities with what are sometimes referred to as the "golden rules of accounting," which treat every transaction as individual mutually exclusive events, this principle fundamentally requires the separate capture and unintrusive storage of every respective interaction. Its underlying premise enables sustainable outcome consistency as well as perpetual transactional integrity.

TIMESTAMP SEPARATION, THE PRINCIPLE OF

Hinged on the fact that state changes are not always known at the point from which they become effective, this principle resolves this conundrum by its separate immutable ingestion of each individual point in time. This approach to separating the point of effectiveness from the point of knowledge – for each individual event – achieves the best of both worlds, reduces friction and enables associative flexibility.

NATURAL GRANULARITY, THE PRINCIPLE OF

One of the most powerful attributes of data is its ability to enable recombinant innovation. This power to restate, reanalyse or recombine data is significantly enhanced when the raw and natural state of data is preserved: the underlying imperative of the principle of natural granularity. Its implication is that every event, every interaction and every transaction is individually captured and is immutably preserved – with every raw data point kept materially identical to its true state at its point of capture.

INTENTIONAL SILOS, THE PRINCIPLE OF

Much like the methodology used for the design and architecture of microservices, the approach underpinned by this principle is a focus on breaking big things into smaller units. At its core, it is an important enabler for delivering new data products or services – or for applying changes to old ones – at pace. It also allows an appropriate level of separation for an individual product or service to be designed, developed, managed and scaled independently of all others.

BIOLOGICAL DATA LINKS, THE PRINCIPLE OF

Rather than promoting the use of synthetic keys, the principle of biological data links advocates the construction of sustainable links between disparate data sets by the conjunction of immutable natural keys with naturally immutable event timestamps. Placing significant reliance on the combination of *the principle of timestamp separation* with *the principle of immutability by design*, it helps to reduce complexities of dependency management and latencies within data pipelines.

BACKWARD COMPATIBILITY, THE PRINCIPLE OF

The principle of backward compatibility is an approach to ensure that new things do not have adverse impacts on old things. By perpetually preserving the structural integrity of defined data structures, this principle helps to reduce complexities of change while increasing code deployment flexibility.

SMOKE AND MIRRORS, THE PRINCIPLE OF

To enable seamless transformations – from the delivery of small data products to such large initiatives as sizable shifts towards the cloud – it is additionally essential to establish a transition-friendly hybrid architecture. The principle of smoke and mirrors provides a framework for delivering logical abstractions that enable increased flexibility and adaptability of underlying physical data structures. This principle's technical implementation can often be achieved employing combinations of layers of service endpoints, customised views and creative metadata.

Index

A

academics
 Frederic Mishkin, 10
 professor David Vanhoose, 40
 professor Iftekhar Hasan, 40
 professor Muir, 120
 professor Niall Ferguson, 27
 professor Yehning Chen, 40
AI
 data and capabilities, 108
 data and investments, 108
 models, 182
 and technology solutions, 136
analysis
 contingency, 24
 data, 22, 34, 148
 descriptive, 34
 meticulous, 40
 modelled, 32
 novel, 24
 by Our World in Data, 177
 and reports, 32
 resultant, 180
 revealed, 137
 root cause analysis (RCA), 56, 120
 statistical, 150
 of trend, 148
architecture
 bottleneck, 109
 data, 62, 149
 and design approaches, 133
 enterprise, 108
 hybrid, 158, 191
 micro services, 60, 158, 190
 role, 63
 service-oriented, 73
 system, 188
 team, 109, 141
 technology, 73, 135
 transitional, 135, 152

artificial intelligence
 advancements in, 6
 analytics and, 97, 99
 big data and, 91
 data and, 93, 107, 139, 157, 172
 data foundation for, 71
 data science and, 54, 59, 148
 machine learning and, 63, 93
 powered by, 49, 52
 power of, 154
 solution, 182
 transformation, 89

C

change
 addressing bottlenecks, 20
 circles of, 60
 in circumstance, 148
 complexities, 158, 191
 data, 139–140, 148
 inability to, 61
 to legacy, 20
 missed opportunities, 57
 organisational, 12, 59, 71, 187
 pace of, 64, 108, 155
 paradigm shift, 16, 54, 62, 64, 132, 154,
  163–164
 proponents of, 12
 radical, 37, 62, 66, 98, 146
 rapid, 51
 roadmap for, 163
 of roles, 61
 scale of, 134
 speed of, xxi, 29, 93, 95, 113, 166
 speed of execution, 64, 93
 tangible, 59
 transformational, 90
concerns
 about disharmonious interactions, 164
 about potential impacts, 70

Printed in the United States
by Baker & Taylor Publisher Services

Printed in the United States
by Baker & Taylor Publisher Services